HELLGATE BOOKS
— IRAQ WAR —

CHARLIE BATTERY

✳ ✳ ✳

A MARINE ARTILLERY UNIT IN IRAQ

Andrew Lubin

Hellgate Press
Central Point, OR

CHARLIE BATTERY
A MARNE ARTILLERY UNIT IN IRAQ

© 2004 by Andrew Lubin
Published by Hellgate Press

Hellgate Press
a division of PSI Research
P.O. Box 3727
Central Point, OR 97502-0032
info@psi-research.com *e-mail*

Editor: Vickie Reierson
Book designer: Constance C. Dickinson
Compositor: Jan O. Olsson
Cover designer: Lynn Dragonette

Library of Congress Cataloging-in-Publication Data

Lubin, Andrew.
  Charlie Battery : a Marine artillery unit in Iraq / Andrew Lubin.
    p. cm.
  Includes bibliographical references.
  ISBN 1-55571-642-3
  1. Iraq War, 2003. 2. United States. Marine Corps. Marines, 21st C
Battery. 3. United States—History, Military—20th century. I. Title.

  DS79.76.L83 2003
  956.7044'342—dc22

                                                2004015330

Printed and bound in the United States of America
First edition 10 9 8 7 6 5 4 3 2 1

 Printed on recycled paper when available.

As they are part of 228 years of Marine history and tradition, let me mention three Marines who have played such an important part in my life:

Captain James L. Lubin

Corporal Claire M. Lubin

Lance Corporal Philip James Lubin

Mom and Dad, I learned about Marine tradition and history from you both, and Phil, now I have the privilege of watching you add to it.

Contents

Prologue

I was driving to work on Thursday morning, January 9, when my cell phone rang. Looking down at the screen, I saw the caller was my son, Philip. "Good morning, Phil," I answered. "What's up?" He (and most of the Marine Corps) had been recalled from their holiday leave on New Year's Day, in order to participate in Operation Enduring Freedom, and he was calling me from his barracks in Camp Lejeune. It was increasingly obvious that the United States was going to go to war against Iraq, so Phil and I had been discussing my visiting him sometime in late January before he deployed. I assumed I was about to get an update on his unit's packing and loading status. Instead, his voice sounded strained and he was speaking too fast. "Dad, you've got to come down sooner than we thought ... the Word just came down ... I'm leaving Saturday. Can you come down today?"

He didn't have to ask me twice, and I assured him I'd be there to see him before he sailed. As I hung up the phone, a thousand thoughts ran through my mind, the first of which were all practical. Phil was stationed at Camp Lejeune, North Carolina, a 10-hour drive from our home in Pennsylvania. Did the car need an oil change, or any work? How much cash would I need? What about a hotel reservation? Would his mother want to come along? These questions, along with similar fatherly practical problems, were ones I'd either resolve quickly or on the drive south. At the same time, however, I began hearing another voice, on a deeper level, that kept saying to me, "This is no longer a TV advertisement. My son is a Marine and going off to war." Added to this thought was the unspoken one: "What if he gets killed?"

The practical problems were easily handled. The car was ready for a long trip, I'd book a hotel room from the highway, and I'd stop at an ATM later that day. My job is in sales and marketing, so all I had to do was bring my telephone diary; I could make my calls from the road.

The only other question was when would I leave? After Phil and I talked a few more times during the morning, he thought he would be working that day, part of the evening, and probably through noon the next day. So we decided I'd spend Thursday working and getting ready for the trip, and then leave Friday in the early morning hours. That would let me arrive at Camp Lejeune approximately when he was getting off duty, and he and I would have Friday afternoon, Friday night, and any time Saturday that the Marine Corps would allow us. Phil seemed relieved to know I'd come down before he left; it never occurred to me not to see him off.

Phil called me again that evening to tell me there were no last-minute hitches in his work schedule, so our plans to meet in the early afternoon remained unchanged. He said he'd leave a pass for me at the main gate, and then gave me directions to his barracks, along with a new directional aid of his generation: "If you have a problem, Dad, just call me on my cell."

Getting out of bed at 0300 was easy—I was anxious to be on the road and driving. Fortunately, there was little-to-no traffic that day, so other than a quick head call when I crossed the Potomac River into Virginia and a stop for gas in North Carolina, the trip was totally uneventful, and I pulled up to the Camp Lejeune main gate by 1330.

While the cable stations, newspapers, and television talk shows were full of war news—what would the UN do? What about the French, Bush, and Saddam?—I was unprepared for the war readiness and bustle in and around the base. The guards at the gate were armed and flak-jacketed, and extra Marines with M16s stood alertly off to the side, eyeballing everyone driving through the gates. MPs blocked traffic as long convoys rumbled out of Lejeune. I counted three long convoys, 20 to 30 vehicles long, as I waited at the gate.

The jingoistic, rah-rah attitude pushed by Fox News hadn't reached the gates of Camp Lejeune; all I saw were grim-looking, heavily armed, busy, dirty Marines loading their gear and getting ready for battle, as thousands of Marines over the years had done before them. It would have made for the beginning of an excellent war movie, except that this time, it wasn't John Wayne in his old movie, "Sands of Iwo Jima." The next day, my son was leaving with them.

There seemed to be a disconnect between what I was feeling and seeing, as compared to the attitude in the rest of the United States. When I called my office that Thursday morning and told my boss where I was going and why, his attitude seemed oddly neutral. Of course he understood why I was going, but otherwise, his greatest concern was that I make my sales calls from the road.

No one I talked to during my drive to Camp Lejeune seemed to have any sense of urgency or importance in our sending troops to Iraq. Perhaps most people didn't really see a need to send troops to depose Saddam, perhaps without a son in the service, they felt no real connection with what was happening—or perhaps I wanted people to say, "Your son is a Marine? Congratulations! Good luck to him, and is there anything we can do?" I began to viscerally understand the divisions and rifts that appeared in America in the late 1960s and early 1970s when our troops were fighting in Vietnam; at the very least, I wasn't happy with the current American attitude.

Between asking the Marine at the guard shack, and Phil's directions from the night before, I found his barracks on N Street quickly. I'd called him when I cleared the guard shack, so he was waiting for me on the street when I drove up. Among the Marines loading and driving Humvees and trucks, and the other Marines loading containers and moving towed artillery, I spotted Phil easily. He'd only graduated from boot camp six months earlier, so despite the muscles, the cammies, the tattoos, and his short Marine haircut, he looked to be the same goofy kid I'd driven to soccer games, taken to school, and dropped off at the mall. I hadn't yet made the mental switch where he'd changed from "Phil, my kid" to "Phil, my son the Marine," but on this day, he was growing up before my eyes.

I had no set plan for the day; whatever he needed to do, or wanted to do, was fine with me. I also wanted Phil to know any friends he wanted to invite along were equally welcome because I didn't want any of them to be alone. Initially, it was awkward; Phil was uptight and tense, and frankly, I was nervous. I didn't know what he wanted or what he needed, and it was frustrating to not be able to help him immediately. So, we did what many families do these days for activity; we drove to the mall after getting him a Marine haircut.

Of course, a mall outside a Marine base isn't exactly the same as a typical mall elsewhere. Although the Jacksonville Mall had the usual stores for CDs, clothing, and greeting cards, it also had one that sold Marine clothing and dogtags, which was where we went shopping. Phil needed extra dogtags and, as he explained it to me, a Marine in combat is required to wear three: two around his neck and the remaining one laced into his left boot should he be caught in a mortar blast or hit by an artillery shell and blown apart, the theory was they could identify him from the dogtag in his boot, or if he was killed "normally," they'd shove one of the two from around his neck between his teeth. Just lovely.

As the afternoon progressed, both he and I began to unwind and relax. Our talk revolved around more normal topics—his mother, his cat, and his friends back home—that was more of how I'd hoped the day would go.

Back at the barracks, Phil laughed thinking I was too old to lift his pack and gear (a combat load), and I'd need his help to put his pack on. Fortunately, he was wrong, and while I did swing his pack up and onto my back, it was noticeably not as graceful a maneuver as when he did it.

With his roommate already forwarded to the ship, and Phil having packed away his personal gear, his barracks room was stark and impersonal. Normal items, such as posters, phones, computers, and TVs, all had been packed away by each Marine earlier in the week, and it was time for us to begin to get serious and bring his gear to the Motor Pool. Night had fallen by the time we made our way to the Motor Pool, and in fact, it was closed. But Phil talked to the Marine who was standing guard, and he unlocked the gate and let us in. In the dark, it was a forbidding scene. The parking lot was filled with lines of M198 155mm howitzers, Humvees, and 7-ton trucks. They were all stuffed with gear and equipment awaiting their ride to the port the next day. An olive-drab military Humvee is a far different-looking vehicle than the one advertised on television. Loaded with helmets, gear, and seabags, and parked next to a howitzer, it is a large and lethal sight. We found his vehicle without too much difficulty, and loaded his pack, seabag, and flak jacket in the back. Phil's major concern was whether he was riding with his Battery Gunny (gunnery sergeant), and that God forbid, he might have to talk with him. Be it an issue of rank or age, he was more comfortable riding with his friends.

While at the Motor Pool, Phil surprised me. "Do you see this building?" he asked, pointing to a nearby office structure. "That's where Grandpa worked. I go in there all the time, and I know where he worked, and maybe which desk was his." He floored me with his flood of knowledge and information about my father's career in the Marine Corps. My father had served in both World War II and Korea, and retired as a captain in 1952. I knew bits and pieces of what he'd done, and had written away for his service records in order to find out more. When they arrived, I was in the midst of some business problems, so I'd simply given them to Phil. My father and Phil were very close; he was my parents' first grandchild, and his death, on Phil's tenth birthday, was devastating for my son. So for me to learn that Phil had searched out where his grandfather served (and to learn he commanded the same Motor Pool some 55 years ago!) was a very pleasant surprise.

The restaurants outside of Camp Lejeune were packed that Friday night with Marines of all ages with their families, parents, spouses, and children; we stopped at three separate places before we found a restaurant with less than an hour's wait. While crowded, the mood in each was subdued; no one had driven to Camp Lejeune to celebrate a son or daughter leaving for the upcoming war with Iraq. However, our dinner was relatively lively, especially after Phil was served a few drinks without being asked for ID. (He'd managed to quote the old Vietnam-era saying, "If I'm old enough to fight, I'm old enough to drink," at least twice.) That evening, no one argued his point. He tried to pick-up the waitress by mentioning it might be his last night in the USA for quite some time. It probably wasn't the first time she'd heard that line that evening, and she laughed pleasantly, wished him luck, and went to wait on another table.

Meanwhile, I sipped my drink and listened to my son talk about how well trained he was, what a great team he and his friends were on his gun, and how he had just been selected for .50-caliber machine gun training and been designated as his unit's nuclear, biological, chemical (NBC) expert. It struck me that despite my divorce from his mother, his grandfather's death, and all the angst and confusion so in vogue for his generation, my son had turned into a very fine young man, and it was a pleasure just sitting with and listening to him.

The bustle of deployment had slowed when we returned to his barracks after dinner. USS *Ashland*, was already docked at Morehead

City, and most of his friends had left for the ship; in fact, there were only a few Marines still on the entire second floor. Two of his friends, Lance Corporal Carl Warren and Corporal Jamie Keane, wandered by to say hello; I'd brought some beer and cigars for Phil and any of his friends, so we all stood outside, drank, smoked, and chatted. Phil told them how we'd gone to the Motor Pool to load his gear, and how he'd shown me his grandfather's office. They were amazed; he'd not told them that his grandfather was a Marine officer and had commanded this unit. Keane had armory duty that evening, so around midnight we all shook hands, and I wished them both good luck and a safe return, and they left.

It was quiet on the base, and even quieter now in Phil's room. I made sure he had addresses of family and friends, as well as writing paper, stamps, and some extra pens. Then Phil handed me his extra dogtag, and as I held it in my hand, he said, "You don't hold them, Dad, you wear them." As I slipped it around my neck, I could see him visibly relax. It was an awkward moment; we both knew that it was time for me to leave, yet both of us were reluctant to say it out loud. Despite knowing he'd probably decline, I suggested he come back and stay at the Microtel with me, and that I'd bring him back in the morning. I was correct; Phil said it was time for him to get some sleep; he had to be up at 0400 to report to the armory to have his M16 and bayonet issued.

So I stood up and told him that it was time for me to go. Phil stood up also, and said he was glad I'd come down to see him off. We looked at each other and I gave him a hug and a kiss on the top of his head. I told him I loved him, to remember Grandpa, and do a good job—and that I'd be there to greet him when he returned.

Then it was time for me to turn and walk away.

Introduction

This is an easy story for me to write. All I have to do is act as the narrator; interview some very interesting and dedicated young men, and then write (and try to clean up) the stories they've told me about their war.

This is the story of 21 United States Marines from 2nd Marine Division, 1/10, C Battery. They are part of an artillery battery based in Camp Lejeune, North Carolina. C Battery (Charlie) consists of 55 officers, senior NCOs, and enlisted men who fire six large M198 155mm howitzers. The youngest of them all was my son, Lance Corporal Philip Lubin (age 19 when they left in January 2003), and the oldest was 1st Sergeant Michael Winstead (age 39). They hailed from all corners of the United States, a few were from other countries, including Zaire and England. Without the Marine Corps, their paths may never have crossed nor would they have become friends.

I'm luckier than most parents. I have a career that allows me to make my own hours, so when Phil called me on January 9, 2003, I was able to respond. But many parents don't have that kind of flexibility. For example, Corporal Gaspar Aguila is from Portland, Oregon; his mother couldn't get away on a no-notice basis. The same was true for Corporal Mike Czombos' father, who lives in Youngstown, Ohio—a 13-hour drive from Camp Lejeune. Let me assure you that if Paul Czombos had the same job flexibility, he would have raced me to Camp Lejeune's front gate to be pier-side when his son sailed off to war.

This book is not a political story. George W. Bush, Donald Rumsfeld and the question of weapons of mass destruction (WMD) don't get debated. With elections and political posturing always on the horizon, others will write about and report on the increasingly partisan politics of this war. While interesting, those politics are unimportant to this story. My interest—and the interest and concerns of all the Charlie Battery parents, spouses, and children—was the safe return of our sons and husbands.

But the Charlie Battery story is probably not as simple as I'd like to portray it. On a larger scale, what was initially unimportant to me and the other parents and wives, is far more important to our American way of life than we realized on that blustery January day when they all sailed away. It is important to try to understand that special breed of person who becomes a Marine, and is therefore ready to answer America's call. Regardless of how you view the rationale for the war—be it because of 9/11, Saddam Hussein's tyranny, the threat of weapons of mass destruction, or none of these—it was still my son and his friends who were being sent overseas to fight, and therefore, it is worth asking these Marines, our sons and husbands, about how they felt being the tip of our American spear.

It's the lure of being involved in these stories, when added to being the tip of the American spear, that makes being a Marine so exciting. Most good Marine recruiters will point out to their recruits that since November 10, 1775, the Marines have been America's primary retaliatory force. Indeed, the expression, "Send in the Marines," was coined in the early 1900s, and has remained popular ever since. As Max Boot writes in his book, *The Savage Wars of Peace*, the Marines have been America's major (and quiet) method of projecting our power throughout the world. From Stephan Decatur in Tripoli (1804) to Smedley Butler in the Boxer Rebellion (China, 1900) to Herman Hannekin and Dan Daily in the Central American Banana Wars (Haiti, 1919) and Chesty Puller in Nicaragua (1932), it has been the Marines who have quietly enforced the foreign policy decisions of virtually all our presidents.

In 228 years of legendary courage and tradition—from "the halls of Montezuma to the shores of Tripoli," and then on to Belleau Wood, Iwo Jima, and the Chosun Reservoir, the world has effectively learned that if you mess with the United States, you mess with the Marines—which is to your detriment.

Despite the current excitement over high-tech American equipment, and casualty-free warfare, this war has again enhanced the Marine Corps reputation for courage and bravery. While America and the world "oohed and ahhed" at the images of smart bombs blowing out either the left or right palace window from

40,000 feet up, let's not forget how many of the parents and spouses of Charlie Battery stayed awake that nasty March night watching MSNBC "live" as their men helped win the Battle of An Nasiriyah.

B-52s don't pacify villages and then give out candy to children; it's Marines on the ground—like our Marines of Charlie Battery—who do. So at this point, I have the honor of presenting their story. Gentlemen of Charlie Battery, it's time for you to rock and roll!

Charlie Battery: Enlisted Men
Corporal (Cpl.) Gaspar Aguila, Portland, OR
Private (Pvt.) Paul Barr, Harrisonburg, VA
Lance Corporal (LCpl.) Sobola Bechu, Kisangani, Zaire
Corporal (Cpl.) Michael Czombos, Youngstown, OH
Corporal (Cpl.) Jorge Delarosa, Tampa, FL
Corporal (Cpl.) Ryan Gallagher, Delran, NJ
Corporal (Cpl.) Christopher Gault, Pittsburgh, PA
Corporal (Cpl.) Geoffrey Goodson, Weatherford, TX
Corporal (Cpl.) Cory Hebert, Chippewa Falls, WI
Lance Corporal (LCpl.) Joshua Jones, Mount Ida, AR
Lance Corporal (LCpl.) Nicholas Lamb, Portsmouth, VA
Lance Corporal (LCpl.) Philip Lubin, Morrisville, PA
Corporal (Cpl.) Justin Noyes, Vinita, OK
Petty Officer Third Class (PO3) James "Doc" Sanders, U.S. Navy, Houston, TX
Corporal (Cpl.) Joshua Souza, Worcester, MA
Lance Corporal (LCpl.) Joseph Turcotte, Manchester, NH
Lance Corporal (LCpl.) Carl Warren, Baltimore, MD

Charlie Battery Officer & Non-Commissioned Officers (NCOs)
Staff Sergeant (SSgt.) John Fontenoy, Phillipsburg, PA
Gunnery Sergeant (GySgt.) Clay Lambert, Jennings, FL
First Lieutenant (1st Lt.) Sean Shea, Richmond, VA

HQ Battery, 1st Battalion, Tenth Marines (1/10)
Lieutenant Commander (LCDR) Gordon "Chaps" Ritchie, U.S. Navy, Battle Creek, MI
Master Sergeant (MSgt.) Michael Santivasci, Virginia Beach, VA

Charlie Battery's Place in Task Force Tarawa

Task Force Tarawa
BGen. R. Natonski

Regimental Combat Team 2
Col. R. Bailey

Headquarters Company Battalions
1/2 Infantry – Lt. Col. R. Grabowski
3/2 Infantry – Lt. Col. P. Dunahoe
2/8 Infantry – Lt. Col. R. Mortensen
A Company – 2nd Combat Engineers
A Company – 8th Tank
C Company – 2nd LAR
C Company – 2nd Amphibious Assault
1/10

1st Battalion, Tenth Marines
Lt. Col. G. T. Starnes

Alpha Battery	Bravo Battery	Charlie Battery	HQ Battery
		CO: Capt. M. Woodhead	Msgt. M. Santivasci
		Assistant Executive Officer: 1st Lt. S. Shea	
		1st Sgt. M. Winstead	
		GySgt. C. Lambert	
		SSgt. J. Fontenoy	
		SSgt. J. Twiggs	
		PO-3 J. Sanders	

Gun #1	Gun #2	Gun #3	Gun #4	Gun #5	Gun #6
Cpl. J. Souza					
Cpl. G. Aguila	Gallagher	Gault		Czombos	
Cpl. G. Goodson					
Cpl. C. Hebert					
Cpl. J. Wilson					
LCpl. S. Bechu					
LCpl. N. Lamb					
LCpl. P. Lubin					
LCpl. J. Turcotte					
LCpl. C. Warren					

Chapter 1

Meet the Marines

Why They Join

Every Marine has his or her reasons for joining the Corps, and while each and every story reveals a personal history, significant event, or major influence, the stories of a "few good men" in Charlie Battery 1/10 reflect a sampling of just why so many young people decide to join the Marines.

Wanting to Do More

In February 2002, Phil and I were watching the movie "Black Hawk Down," a great father-and-son movie. Early in the movie, there was a scene where a few of the Army Rangers were jogging around their camp, and several others were taking M16 practice. I turned to him and said, "These guys are your age, Phil. You could be doing this." To my absolute surprise, he replied, "We need to talk after the movie, Dad. I'm dying here. I need to get out."

We talked after the movie, and he told me how he hated college, how he wasn't happy with his current part-time job as a cook, and how he wasn't where he wanted to be in his life. He then picked my brain about what I thought of the four service branches. (He'd already thought this out himself; I think I was just re-affirming his own ideas.) The next day, he and I drove to the Marine recruiting office at Oxford Valley Mall. "I needed to do something to make me 'me,'" he said.

Corporal Gaspar Aguila joined up for the same sort of reasons as Phil. Born in Mexico, he and his family moved to America when he was seven. After four years in a nondescript high school, he was foreman in a shop, on an hourly salary, with no particular future. In the Marine Corps, he could travel and see the world, and more importantly, "I had a chance to see what I could do to make something of my life."

Perhaps not surprisingly, this same feeling of restlessness and a need for accomplishment is felt overseas. As LCpl. Sobola Bechu related to me, "I came to this country as a refugee from Zaire. We had an opportunity to do better here. I'd never heard of the Marines Corps when I was in Zaire, but when I got here, in high school, it seemed to me that the Marines would give me an opportunity to give something back to America, and at the same time, give me the chance to be one of the world's very best."

The Marine Corps' reputation for valor and heroism is certainly an attraction to a young man and woman—who doesn't get goose bumps at a picture of the flag raising on Iwo Jima, or the story of the Marines marching out of Chosin Reservoir? However, it is important to point out that these boys in Charlie Battery, normally disinterested in school (but not due to a lack of intelligence) all intrinsically understood the concept that the Marines—in exchange for their sweat, and 150% dedication for the next four years—would give them the opportunity to succeed. They knew the Marine Corps would help them find the necessary spark within themselves to make them want to succeed, be it in battle or back in civilian life.

Corporal Michael Czombos explained, "The Marines have a reputation for getting people's lives squared away." He had experienced some trouble at school, but had always been interested in the military, so joining the Marines made a lot of sense. And they were going to pay him to learn how to shoot and blow things up. "They're absolutely the baddest mother-fucking branch of service there is! But most important, I wanted to earn the title, 'Marine' and make my father proud of me."

> The Marines have a reputation for getting people's lives squared away ...
>
> *Cpl. Michael Czombos*

It's interesting, that from throughout the country, and from around the world, the Marine Corps attracts these under-motivated, yet frustrated young people. It's like a quiet magnetic current that attracts these boys to volunteer the next four years of their lives to the Marines. And the young men and women turn up in droves to enlist. The Marine Corps is the only branch of the service that annually turns people away. Unlike the Army, the Marine Corps does not have to resort to paying people in order to induce them to join up.

Family Tradition

One reason why the Marines don't have as much trouble recruiting is because many young people are following a family tradition.

Private Paul Barr hails from Virginia, which has its own hallowed traditions of family and honor, and has a father who was a Marine and who served in Vietnam. "This is a family tradition! I wasn't so interested in studying, so I signed up in high school for the Marine's Delayed Entry Program. I enlisted only a few days after I graduated." Likewise, Cpl. Geoff Goodson, who is from Texas. His father is a former Marine, and there was little doubt he would not follow in his father's footsteps. As his mother, Sharon, confirmed, "There was never any question that Geoff was going to become a Marine."

Master Sergeant Michael Santivasci enlisted directly from high school as well. His father was career Navy and served for 26 years. His military duties kept his father away quite a lot, and on one occasion, when his mother traveled with the family to Italy on a MAC flight to see him, a seven-year-old Michael saw a Marine in his dress blues playing reveille. "I just thought that being a Marine was the coolest thing. I enlisted right after high school, and I can't imagine doing anything else."

Chaplain Gordon "Chaps" Ritchie had ministered for nine years in Indiana and Iowa before he had a second calling and he decided to join the Navy. He ministers to both Marines and the U.S. Coast Guard as well as the U.S. Navy. While he took a totally different path into the Marine Corps, his father was in World War II and he had an older brother stationed in Germany during the Vietnam War. "I just felt that it was time for me to do my part."

Getting Direction

Lance Corporal Joseph Turcotte and Cpl. Joshua Souza had each been Marines for about three years when they got the recall on New Year's Day 2003. Neither was surprised about it, and both were ready to go. "I was so ready for this," admits Souza, "I wanted to do something different and important with my life." Turcotte, who is normally one of the quieter Marines in Charlie Battery, recalled how he was out of school, working, and living on his own when he decided to join up. "My father was apprehensive when I told him what I'd done, probably because he'd been in the Army. But I knew I could get direction and discipline from the Marines, and I joined to make him proud of me."

Another young man who found a sense of direction by joining the Marines was LCpl. Carl Warren from "Bal-more." Warren loves to boast about his friends and hometown, but when he told

From earliest days, being a Marine was all he ever wanted to do.

Sharon Goodson, mother

I wanted to do something different and important with my life.

Cpl. Joshua Souza

his dad he wouldn't be going to college, his father was concerned about what he was going to do with his life. "He told me I had to do something serious, so I didn't waste my life." His father was very sick at the time, and so Warren listened to him. In October 2000, he decided to join the Marines. Sadly, Warren's father was too sick to see him graduate from boot camp, but he did get to see him in his Marine uniform before he died. "It was like he hung on especially in order to see me graduate."

A Career Opportunity

Many Marines make the Corps a life-long career. Petty Officer James (Hank) Sanders (also known as "Doc"), a married man with children, found himself at a dead-end job, with no benefits and less of a future. He joined the Navy and became a corpsman, and then he was assigned to the Marine Corps. "So if I gave the Navy five good years—look at the career opportunities they'd give me in return!"

The Marine Corps Family

The Marine Corps is a family all its own. First Lieutenant Sean Shea is another example of a man who recognized the career opportunities the USMC offered. "I enlisted in 1988 and served in Desert Storm. I was a sergeant when I got out, and then was active in the Reserves. I had a career in law enforcement, but missed the Marines and came back in. This is my life."

Gunnery Sergeant Clay Lambert talked about being from a "little town in northern Florida." He did his first tour in the Marines, eleven years, and then got out, and worked for the Florida Department of Corrections. But he missed the Marine Corps and being a Marine. He'd fought in Desert Storm and been in Okinawa, Thailand, Korea, and the Philippines. "I've been in the Marine Corps since I was 17; this is my home."

Regardless of regional, educational, or economic background, every Marine is a volunteer who has survived the rigors of boot camp. In every day of training—from classroom to field operations—each has learned to depend on his fellow Marines. Even in the packing and repacking of gear, this trust is important—to forget to pack certain gear, or to pack inferior or faulty gear, could easily cost Marine lives, and that is simply not acceptable.

The military would give me a chance to travel and see the world, but most important, joining the Marines gave me a chance to serve and protect my country.

Cpl. Cory Hebert

He, the Marine, is the decendent of a line of heroes, the bearer of a name hailed as foremost in the annals his country, the custodian of a long cherished reputation for honor, valor, and integrity.

MajGen. John A. Lejeune
13th Commandant, 1922

Where They Fit into Task Force Tarawa

Task Force Tarawa, properly known as Amphibious Task Force East (ATF East), consisted of 7,000 Marines on seven ships: three amphibious assault ships, USS *Kearsarge*, USS *Saipan*, and USS *Bataan*; three landing ship docks (LSDs): USS *Ashland*, USS *Gunston Hall*, and USS *Portland*; and the amphibious transport dock (LDP), USS *Ponce*.

To get a clearer picture of where Charlie Battery fits into this huge floating population, see the chart Charlie Battery's Place in Task Force Tarawa at the end of the Introduction.

The Gun Crew

From boot camp onward, Marines train constantly. Be they infantry, artillery, tankers, or engineers, it is no exaggeration to say that no military unit on earth is as well-trained on a day-to-day level, as your average Marine platoon. Between the physical training (PT) to weapons training, to classroom and academic training, the Marines of Camp Lejeune, Quantico, Camp Pendleton, and elsewhere, are always in a forward motion.

While a battle is nothing if not a fluid and confused situation, the Marine Corps makes their training as realistic as possible. In this way, the Marines would hopefully encounter fewer unknown situations, which would help keep confusion and fear to the minimum level possible. Regardless of whether they are in artillery, armor, or infantry, every member of a Marine squad is both highly trained and cross-trained. Should a Marine on a gun be injured or killed, the unit still is fully functional and operational.

An M198 155mm howitzer is served by a team of eight to eleven Marines. This gun crew works to load, aim, and fire the gun in a very precisely organized and choreographed manner. To get to their mission site, the gun is towed (and defended) by a 7-ton truck with a .50 cal. machine gun in the ring mount, and is accompanied by yet another 7-ton ammo truck, which carries the shells, charges, and fuses for each gun.

How involved is the setting up, aiming, loading, and firing of an M198 155mm howitzer? Let the Marine gun crew of Gun #1 describe how it is properly (the Marine way) done.

Gun #1 of Charlie Battery

No. 1 Man (Plugger), Cpl. Josh Souza

Souza loads the gun by putting the shell in the breech, closing the breech, then putting in the primer. The crew fires when the section chief says to do so. On that command, he pulls the lanyard. After the gun fires, he opens and swabs the breech. Souza also drives the 7-ton truck that pulls the gun. "Those Marines who don't pull the lanyard correctly are known as '2-pump chumps.' I'm not one of them."

No. 2 Man ("A" Gunner), LCpl. Sobola Bechu

Bechu is responsible for elevating and depressing the gun's barrel. The "A" gunner works a handwheel that elevates or depresses the barrel, as per the range requirements. While it sounds simple, the barrel of a 155mm weighs several thousand pounds, so to raise and lower it manually involves turning the handle rapidly for dozens of revolutions.

No. 3 Man (Gunner), Cpl. Jamie Wilson

Although Wilson was section chief-qualified, in the war, he was tasked as the gunner, operating under SSgt. John Twiggs. A gunner makes sure the gun is laid on the proper azimuth of fire both safely and quickly. He is also responsible for the traverse (right to left). The section chief, SSgt. Twiggs, verifies that what the recorder wrote is correct, as well as verifies that the quadrant elevation and traverse entered on the gun is correct, and that the proper round and charge has been loaded. Only then does he give the order for the plugger to fire.

No. 4 Man (Recorder), LCpl. Philip Lubin

When the fire direction control (FDC) calls the mission, the recorder writes it down. Lubin records the coordinates of mission, which shell, which charge, which round, and which fuse. Section Chief Twiggs then verifies what he has written down as correct, and then verifies and coordinates elevation, traverse, round, and charge. Lubin then calls out the round, charge, and fuse requirements to the ammo team.

No. 5 Man (Ammo Tech Chief), Cpl. Cory Hebert

The ammo tech chief (ATC) supervises and assists the Marines pulling the ammunition from the ammo truck to the gun. Hebert keeps track of how many shells, fuses, powder charges, and primers have been used, and/or are available for use. He also ensures that the fuse and round combinations are correct.

No. 6 Man (Ammo Team), LCpl. Carl Warren

Warren puts the proper fuse on the round, and along with LCpl. Turcotte, helps load the shell—after it's properly charged and fused—into the gun. He also is tasked with using the ramming staff to push the round off the loading tray into the gun.

No. 7 Man (Powder Man), LCpl. Joseph Turcotte

After getting the powder charge and fuse information from LCpl. Lubin, he pulls the proper powder charge from the truck, and then gives it to the No. 1 man who loads it into the breach. Turcotte helps him pull the shell from the ammo truck, and gives it to the plugger for loading. Lubin must yell out the details so he can be heard over all the noise. Then, Turcotte sets the proper charge—there are several different charges with several sizes of each.

No. 8 Man (Ground Guide), Cpl. Gaspar Aguila

Aguila works with the section chief on siting and laying the gun at the next position. In battle, he handles the security, or defense, of

Cpl. Gaspar Aguila with .50 caliber machine gun

his gun. "I man the .50 cal. machine gun in the truck ring mount, or otherwise help out as necessary. I helped man the crew-served weapons on the berm, and helped the ammo team, or wherever they needed me most."

Charlie Battery Gun Support Team

While these Marines fire their howitzers at an optimum rate of four rounds per minute (up to six per minute with their adrenaline flowing in battle), there are other Marines in Charlie Battery who are equally important for the smooth operation of the gun crew in the confusion of battle.

Fire Direction Control (FDC), LCpl. Nicholas Lamb

Lamb receives the mission coordinates from the forward observers (FOs), who are usually spotted several miles forward, with the infantry. The FDC is stationed some 100 meters behind the gun line, and relays the mission coordinates, including which type of shell and which charge, to the recorder. He passes this information to the recorder by "either voice or computer. It's a digital system. Speed and accuracy are important. On a Red Rain mission—where our radar tracks incoming mortars, artillery, or rockets—I need to get the mission coordinates from our FOs to the recorders and his gun crews ASAP!"

Corpsman James "Doc" Sanders

Corpsman, PO3 James "Doc" Sanders

Sanders is the chief corpsman for Charlie Battery. He is fully versed and trained in all battlefield wounds, as well as nuclear, biological, chemical (NBC) situations, and triage. "I also know how to shoot. I'm Navy, but I can do whatever it takes to protect my Marines."

Driver, Cpl. Geoffrey Goodson

Goodson is Humvee-qualified, so he drives 1st Lt. Shea. "Since I'm at his call, it's my job to stay close to him, unless I'm needed for something else." He is .50 cal-qualified and can work the ring mount, if necessary. He is also trained to handle all the crew-served weapons.

Battery Officers & NCOs

While a Marine artilleryman is well-trained and able to handle all the roles on his howitzer, he needs to receive his directions and leadership from the battery officers and senior non-commissioned officers (NCOs). These Marines are typically career Marines and have the breadth of knowledge, training, and prior experience that enables them to lead by knowledge and experience.

1st Lt. Sean Shea

Shea's role is to coordinate the orders and missions between Charlie Battery's commanding officer and the senior NCOs who direct each gun. He keeps an eye on the younger Marines, and stays abreast of the physical and mental status of everyone under his command. Having been a sergeant and having seen combat during 1991's Operation Desert Storm, he had the advantage on being able to brief his NCOs on what to expect, so they could in turn instruct their men.

1st Sgt. Michael Winstead

The 1st sergeant advises the commanding officer (CO) as to the overall status of the battery. He keeps current on the medical, physical, and psychological status of the troops, along with their accountabilities.

GySgt. Clay "Gunny" Lambert

The gunnery sergeant keeps the battery operating properly and efficiently. He is the senior cannoneer in the battery and reports to his CO concerning the status of the unit. He has the knowledge and the experience to handle combat situation problems as well as handling all the ammunition, logistical, personnel, support, and maintenance issues. Equally important, the typical gunnery sergeant has at least a ten-year age advantage on most Marine enlisted men. This helps him get his young Marines through any problematic or difficult situations.

SSgt. John Fontenoy

As one of the two staff sergeants in the battery, Fontenoy handles the battery's security. That means he spots and sets the crew-served weapons on the gun line; establishes the best fields of fire; and decides which quadrant is best served by each gun. He assists on advance party (AP) in order to set each gun, and also has the ability to act as a section chief and run a gun, if necessary.

1st Battalion, Tenth Marines (1/10) HQ

As Charley Battery comprised just 6 of the 18 howitzers in 1/10, there is another layer of direction and leadership above 1st Lt. Shea and the Battery CO. This would be the 1/10 Battalion Headquarters.

MSgt. Michael Santivasci

Santivasci is the senior cannoneer; hence, the nickname, "Top," as in "the top sergeant." Having served in both Desert Storm and the Somali mission in 1993, Santivasci deployed as one of the most experienced Marines in the Assault Force East.

He was the field artillery chief of 1/10. With almost 23 years as an 0811 (a cannoneer), he was the right-hand man to Lt. Col. Glenn Starnes. When it came to the readiness of the howitzers, he was responsible for making sure every gun was combat ready, and that the men could put rounds to the ground in a timely manner. This means he is responsible in the maintenance of each gun, checking on all the safety issues, knowing the ammunition status, and coordinating siting and laying each gun with the respective gunnery sergeants for each battery. He also monitored the status of the gun line trucks and related equipment, like the SL-3 components, which include picks and shovels, aiming posts, and sights for the howitzers.

Either at Camp Lejeune or during a deployment like Operation Iraqi Freedom, Santivasci monitors all the battery personnel and makes any recommendations pertaining to the staffing of each gun. It's also his job to advise and assist all the battery gunnery sergeants on any artillery issue that arises, and he acts as a mentor to his gunnery sergeants and the enlisted leadership.

LCDR Gordon "Chaps" Ritchie

As a chaplain, Chaps Ritchie is responsible for the moral and spiritual well-being of all the Marines, both officers and enlisted men. At the time of the deployment, he was the chaplain to the 2nd Marine Division and responsible for providing for the spiritual needs of more than 7,000 Marines, as well as providing moral guidance to the commanding officers.

He also supervises the different battalion chaplains and walks the lines with his chaplains in order to minister to as many individual Marines as he can. "I ride with them, eat the same food as them, and march next to them in the same slop. I served in Desert Storm in 1991 and also spent 13 months in Afghanistan before I shipped out to Iraq in January of 2003. The only difference between me and the Marines is that they carry weapons and I have my cross."

We were well-trained before we left. I remembered how much better prepared we were in Desert Storm than the Iraqis, and I was damn sure we'd be even more ready this time.

GySgt. Clay Lambert

As an integral part of Task Force Tarawa, Charlie Battery—along with its commanding officers—packed off their six guns, with their supporting trucks, Humvees, shells, and personal weapons on USS *Ashland*, and after being recalled to duty on New Year's Day 2003, they continued with their training. But this time, it was on shipboard heading for the Persian Gulf.

Chapter 2

Gearing Up

The Minstrel Boy to the war has gone,
In the ranks of death you will find him.
His father's sword he has girded on,
With his wild harp slung behind him.

Traditional, Irish melody
Early 1600s

Camp Lejeune
1–11 January 2003

New Year's Day 2003 dawned with bittersweet news for most all of Charlie Battery and the rest of the 2nd Marine Division from Camp Lejeune. Prior to the holidays, every Marine had been required to leave emergency contact phone numbers before he or she was released for holiday leave. At the time, Phil told me it was yet one more minor Marine annoyance, but on New Year's Day, Phil and other members of Charlie Battery received calls instructing them to return to Camp Lejeune immediately.

Except for Phil, and two other new members of the battery, all the Charlie Battery Marines had been away for six months on the *Trenton* float (February–August 2002). Being recalled for deployment only four months after they'd just come home was especially painful for them. While on USS *Trenton*, they had sailed through the Middle East and the Subcontinent, where they spent the time visiting and training in Djibouti (a small country near Somalia), the Red Sea, Bahrain, the Seychelles, and other similar areas. A Marine float is where a marine battalion spends time in a selected area while operating on a wartime footing; so most of the Charlie Battery Marines already had practical experience in the Middle East and the Persian Gulf, which would serve them well in the coming months.

Phil had invited one of his friends, LCpl. Josh Jones, home with him for the Christmas holidays. In expectation of an official deployment order, the Marine Corps had put a 600-mile limit on holiday travel. While Phil just sneaked in under this limit, Jones hails from Mt. Ida, Arkansas, so he was too far from home to be allowed to go. Worse, Jones had just returned from the *Trenton* float, so he had not been home for most of 2002.

Lance Corporal Jones and Phil spent Christmas 2002 at Phil's home in Pennsylvania. Jones fit in well and enjoyed his Christmas away from home. They drank beer and went skateboarding, and they each got another tattoo. They'd met some girls and partied, and the girls let them know how impressed they were to be with Marines. The recall ruined a good holiday, but with Iraq all over the news, it didn't come as a total surprise. Like Jones, Cpl. Geoff Goodson never made it back to his home in Texas for the holiday season. Instead, he went to Pvt. Paul Barr's house in Virginia where he hung out with Barr and his girlfriend. "It was cool. We Marines take care of each other."

Interestingly, Marine holiday leave is broken into two sections: 1st and 2nd Block. Thus, a Marine is typically home for either Christmas or New Year's. Several Charlie Battery Marines were, therefore, in Camp Lejeune when they got the recall. Back in the barracks for 2nd Block Leave, Cpl. Gault had to make the call home to his mother himself. "That was a difficult call to make. She was upset; my grandmother was upset; a lot of tears and crying. I wasn't really surprised we were going to ship out, but talking to them that day was hard to do."

Corporal Mike Czombos managed to get home for the holidays, and the call from Camp Lejeune took him totally by surprise. "I didn't really think that we'd be going back to the Middle East, probably because we'd just come back from the float, but I have to admit that our CO did warn us not be surprised if we went out again. I should have paid more attention to the news."

Doc Sanders was ready, perhaps because as a father and a husband, he needed to prepare his family for his probable departure. From October onward, he anticipated being sent to Iraq to fight; it was just a question of when. He'd talked to Becky, his wife, about it, and they both had talked to their girls, who were three and six years old. They knew the girls really didn't understand the details, so they just explained that daddy would be going away for a while.

Some Marines, like Cpl. Hebert, suspected more about what was about to happen than they admitted to family and friends.

Hebert recalled he was with Leah Stander, his fiancée, at her home in Morgantown, West Virginia, when he got the recall notice on New Year's Day. He remembered being warned continually in October and November that things were heating up, and not to be surprised if they got called back. She, however, was unaware of what her fiancé was facing. "He certainly didn't tell me any of that. Cory did his best to keep this away from me, and I was very unpleasantly surprised."

Not far away in Washington D.C., another couple was spending the holiday together. Lance Corporal Bechu and his girlfriend, Laura Doggett, were at a party with friends when the Marine Corps called. Doggett, after reading newspapers and watching television news all that fall, had assumed Bechu would be called soon. Neither of them were surprised when the Marine Corps found Bechu and summoned him back to Camp Lejeune. Doggett added that "We were on-and-off as a couple at that point anyway. We'd been dating three years, and knew each other for longer, so maybe this gave us each time to decide how we felt about each other. But regardless of what happened to us as a couple, I was certainly going to support him when he was away."

> At Christmas, I toasted all the Marines already overseas, and those who were about to go. I didn't know a week later, I'd be one of them!
>
> *LCpl. Joseph Turcotte*

How the Families Reacted to the Recall

Receiving these phone calls are never easy, and they take a particular toll on the mothers and wives of the young Marines. The phone call looking for her son, Carl, devastated Lucille Warren. She had recently lost her husband to cancer just 18 months before, and earlier in December, she had been told of layoffs in her department. "I just didn't know how much more I could take," she confessed. "To have Carl taken away to go to war, after all the other bad times I was going through, was just more than I could bear."

For those veteran wives, the recall notice simply fulfilled their woman's intuition. Lisa Santivasci, wife to MSgt. Santivasci, had been experiencing a premonition since October about her husband being sent back to the Gulf. So when he was called back on December 31—while they were visiting with family in Virginia—she wasn't as upset as many others. "Even though the official word was that they would be gone to an unnamed destination for an undetermined period of time, with what we'd seen on the news all fall, you had to be a moron not to know they were going to Iraq." Similarly, deep down, Christy Fontenoy knew that her husband, SSgt. Fontenoy, would be going back to the Middle East. She did not dwell on it because she'd been a Marine wife long enough to ignore all the daily rumors that seem to circulate through a Marine base. The difficult part was that he'd just come back from the *Trenton* float, and she was pregnant with their second child, and they didn't know how long he'd be gone.

As far back as September 2002, Lasana and Chaps Ritchie discussed his return to action. Since he had just returned from Afghanistan, the Marine Corps offered to transfer him to a battalion that would not be deployed. He told Lasana that it was her call whether or not he should go back, but she told him it was his choice and she would support him either way. Once she said that, it was actually a very simple decision to go back. "These are my Marines, and I had to be with them if they needed me."

Coming Back to Camp Lejeune

As the Charlie Battery Marines and others streamed back to Camp Lejeune on January 2 and 3, their thoughts and concerns were focused on their upcoming deployment, and whether or not they would be called upon to fight. They did not have to worry about the quality of their training, however; that had long been taken care of for them by the Marine Corps, with their world-class facilities at Camp Lejeune.

From the entrance, Camp Lejeune is an unimposing base. As you drive up, the visitor center, where family and friends sign in for their gate passes, is on the right, and to the left, there are two lanes and a guard shack for those with a base pass. It is only when you gain access to the base that you realize just how huge a facility Camp Lejeune is today.

Since the 2nd Marine Division set up a "temporary" camp in the middle of a pine forest in September 1941, this camp has grown in both size and importance to the Marine Corps. Camp Lejeune is now the largest Marine Corps base in the world. As described on the Camp Lejeune website:

> Camp Lejeune is home to more than 47,000 Marines and Sailors from around the world ... they serve with hundreds of company-sized units that compose the 8 major commands headquartered on the base ... units come to train and are then deployed around the globe to fight wars. Today Camp Lejeune boasts 14 miles of beach capable of supporting amphibious training operations ... 54 live-fire ranges, 89 maneuver areas, 33 gun positions, and 25 tactical

> I couldn't make it thru a pre-deployment meeting for the wives. I was too upset thinking about Gaspar going to war.
>
> *Amanda Aguila, wife*

landing zones ... on a 246 square mile training facility. This is one of the world's premier military training facilities ... there are regularly scheduled bilateral and NATO-sponsored exercises.

The 2nd Marine Division's Special History

A Marine leaving Camp Lejeune is not only well-trained for whatever situation he encounters, but he also carries with him the heritage of his specific unit. Marine history and heritage begins in boot camp, where every Marine recruit learns about the battles, heroes, and traditions that preceded him. While every Marine division has its own share of history and heroism behind it, the 2nd Marine Division won their worldwide renown for their incredible performance in the bloody battle of Tarawa on 20–23 November 1943. The 2nd Marine Division took the island of Tarawa, but at a cost of 3,407 casualties. One man died for every three wounded, which reflected the savagery of the fighting. Later, the 2nd Marine Division also fought in other Pacific Theatre actions, as well as in Korea and Vietnam. Charlie Battery was in Beirut in October 1983 when the Marine barracks was bombed, and was later an active participant in Operation Desert Shield/Desert Storm.

While the 2nd Marine Division has as valiant a battle history as every other Marine division, it was for their heroic and determined performance at Tarawa that led the Marine Corps to name this 2nd Division group, "Task Force Tarawa."

Under the assumption that the Iraqis would fight hard to defend their country, and that Charlie Battery would continue the 2nd Marine Division's illustrious history of action and heroism, I had no reason to hope that Charlie Battery's Iraq campaign would be any easier for them than for their renowned predecessors. As the father of a young 2nd Division Marine sailing off to war, knowing Marine Corps history only added to my worries.

I didn't bother sharing these fears with Phil's mother, Jamie McMillan; there was no sense upsetting her more than she was already. Not surprisingly, she was most unhappy about her son leaving. "Phil is my only son, and I'm a single mother, so it was hard for me to accept him leaving when he joined the Marines. I was sure that we would be fighting a war soon, and I knew enough Marine history to know I didn't want to know more. I said my good-byes on New Year's Day, and there was no way I could go through it again."

When I took Joe's ornaments off the tree Jan. 8, it hit me I might have seen him for the last time, and I just cried.

Nancy Turcotte, mother

Marine wife, Lisa Santivasci, struggled with her husband's deployment as well since she had been down that road before. In 1991, she saw her husband deploy for Desert Storm and for Somalia in 1993, but by then the couple had two sons, Michael and Raymond. "We had taken the boys to Field Day, when families are invited to watch what their Marines do. Seeing the batteries firing their 155s helped both boys understand what their dad's job was." After he left for deployment duty, she kept them steady by constantly explaining, "Daddy was away on a training mission, and because he was an awesome Marine and the men he trained were awesome Marines, Daddy would be safe. Then I worried quietly—but not around them."

Staff Sergeant John Fontenoy's wife, Christy, and their son, Cody, found comfort in their church. As a church close to Camp Lejeune, it had approximately 60 Marines deploy, so she was not alone. She also enjoyed a great support system. Between her church, parents, and friends on the base, she could always talk to someone and relieve some of the stress and pressure that would build up thinking about her husband's imminent deployment. "Plus, Cody and I prayed together every morning and evening that the good Lord would keep John safe."

It was this combination of faith in God and Marine training that enabled the wives and parents to maintain their hope that all our Marines would return safely.

Gearing Up for the Invasion

As Charlie Battery Marines packed their personal and battery gear, a subsequent Deployment Order directed the battalion, now tasked to Regimental Combat Team 2 (RCT-2), to embark on the ships that made up Assault Force East. The battalion's men and equipment were loaded onto the task force's ships, with the remaining equipment loaded on two "Assault Follow-on Echelon" ships, USS *Watson* and USS *Redcloud*. As 1st Battalion, Tenth Marines (1/10) was deploying with its 18 M198 155mm howitzers; their Counter Battery Radar Detachment (two radar teams and the Target Processing Center); two bulldozers; two big trailers used to haul equipment; and all the men, ammunition, and spares, the Marines of Charlie Battery worked and loaded their gear into the Assault Force ships on a round-the-clock effort.

Of course, I saw none of this preparation and training during that first week of January. The only ship I saw was the hospital ship, USS *Hope*, from Route 95 as I made my way south to Camp Lejeune that Thursday morning, 9 January. *Hope* was moored in Baltimore Harbor, and I assumed she was deploying soon in order to support the Marines who were shipping out to Iraq. She was riding quietly at anchor, nestled among the car carriers and other cargo ships that one normally sees from the highway. It wasn't the first time I'd seen her, however. I'd visited Ground Zero in New York City a few days after the 9/11 terrorist attack, and saw her tied up off the West Side piers. I remembered reading that *Hope*'s doctors had had nothing to do after the ship arrived; there were no WTC survivors for them to help. Such memories didn't particularly cheer me up as I continued my drive south.

This deployment—with Marines shipping out from both the East Coast (Camp Lejeune) and the West Coast (Camp Pendleton)—was the largest in Marine Corps history. While Operation Desert Storm had been a huge campaign, with hundreds of thousands of soldiers from around the world, Operation Iraqi Freedom was strictly an American and British affair, and it was planned accordingly. The goal was to seize Baghdad as quickly as possible, and in doing so, either kill or depose Saddam Hussein. The Pentagon's thought was that this would destabilize the Iraqi military, and therefore help keep Allied casualties to a minimum. The U.S. Army's V Corps would cross into Iraq from Kuwait, and capture Baghdad from the west, while at the same time, the Marines would send 1st Marine Division (from Camp Pendleton) into Baghdad, running north and west, parallel to the Army.

To accomplish this goal, the Marine Corps created 1st Marine Expeditionary Force (MEF). First MEF was comprised of Task Force Tarawa (from Camp Lejeune), 1st Marine Division, 3rd Marine Air Wing, 1st UK Marine Division, and First Force Service Support Group.

Simply put, Central Command's (Centcom) strategy was for the 1st Marine Division to provide the ground forces needed to seize Baghdad, while Task Force Tarawa and the British Marines would secure the sole Iraqi seaport of Basra, as well as take control of southern Iraq. This included the most important Iraqi city in the south, An Nasiriyah (also known as Nasiriyah).

The road and transportation system in Iraq basically runs north and south, going from the seaport in Basra, through Nasiriyah, through Baghdad, and then dividing to reach Mosul, Tikrit, Kirkuk, and then into Turkey. To accomplish their goal of reaching Baghdad, the Marines would reach the Iraqi highway system by driving cross-country from their assault bases in Kuwait, and intersecting the highway south of Nasiriyah. It was equally essential that Basra and Nasiriyah be captured and secured quickly, and their anti-Saddam Shiite populations pacified, before the expected battles in Baghdad and Saddam's hometown of Tikrit occurred.

But it was the ferocity of the expected battles that was the question of the day—and the answer seemed to depend on which television channel you followed. NBC, ABC, Fox, and CNN all had their own rent-a-generals, all of whom had their own strong and very persuasive opinions on the upcoming war. Depending on which TV military "expert" you followed, the Iraqi Army either would or would not fight aggressively to defend their country. Equally under discussion was whether or not the Iraqi Army would utilize only conventional weapons, or would they escalate the conflict with the vast stocks of chemical weapons, poisonous gasses, and other weapons of mass destruction they were rumored to possess?

To be ready to counter any threat, the Marines knew they would need to bring the necessary stocks of equipment, arms, NBC (nuclear, biological, chemical) gear, armor, munitions, and artillery. While some equipment and troops could quickly be flown overseas, the M198 155mm howitzers, M1 Abrams tanks, 7-ton trucks, and most of the men had to be sent by ship. Since 1/10 was bringing 225 pieces of rolling stock with them, the Marines of Charlie Battery were going to be shipping out in a convoy reminiscent to those of World War II.

Deployment Stages

Back on base, deployment operations consisted of several stages of readiness and work. These are generally spaced over a long period of time, as military readiness is matched to the corresponding political situation, such as Britain's task force cruising slowly to the Falkland Islands in 1981. In view of the speed at which the current world political situation was deteriorating, however, the Marine Corps New Year's Eve recall and deployment was implemented at record pace.

Stage 1 of a normal deployment is Mission Readiness and Rehearsal, where the units involved are trained for their specific tasks. With Charlie Battery being a Marine unit, and most of them having been on a prior float, they returned to Camp Lejeune already fully trained and ready to go.

For Charlie Battery, Stage 2 was easy, if unpleasant. Stage 2 is Pre-Deployment Planning and Readiness, which is primarily a staff and administrative function. As America's quick-response force, the Marine Logistics groups need to have deployment options and situations planned months, if not years in advance, and they do. With pre-positioned equipment (arms, munitions, food, equipment, and all types of spare gear) situated on both vessels and forward bases throughout the world, a Marine Expeditionary Unit (MEU) can arrive at virtually any location in the world ready to fight, and with their supply train already in motion behind them.

Stage 2 Readiness, however, was painful for 1/10 Marines as they stood in lines to receive their anthrax, smallpox, and other shots. As chief corpsman for Charlie Battery, Doc Sanders was responsible for the entire unit's health. Before they shipped out, he confirmed everyone had all their shots, and that they had their complete medical and dental records. If someone had an allergy or a problem with a certain drug, he needed to know about it before combat.

> I got anthrax shots again, and the shots gave me those same huge nasty pimples again.
>
> *Cpl. Justin Noyes*

Sanders administered a variety of shots (anthrax and typhoid), and gave out anti-malaria pills. The small pox shots were saved for the voyage overseas. "I was nauseous after we got our shots," Phil said, "I worked tired and sick to my stomach for days." Even though Cpl. Noyes had been deployed on the *Trenton* float in early 2002, "I got anthrax shots again, and the shots gave me those same huge nasty pimples again."

Then they packed to go off to war.

Deployment Duties

In the days following their return to Camp Lejeune, Charlie Battery worked and packed 18 hours a day. They counted and packed their spare howitzer wheels, welding sets, chains, bolts, and every extra part necessary should one of the guns break in the desert. "It was non-stop work and tension," said SSgt. Fontenoy. "Before we packed, we had to do an inventory and see what we needed. We might have had three tires for a gun, and we needed six, and we had to hustle to find the other three."

> It was a hectic nine days—we all worked pretty hard.
>
> *SSgt. John Fontenoy*

As Charlie Battery was told to prepare to be gone for a tenure of 12 to 18 months, they had to bring enough spare parts and gear with them for the first 30 to 90 days of combat should resupply be impossible or substantially delayed. As such, they packed their gear into the big 20'×40' containers that were being loaded non-stop and shipped off the base.

During these first eight days of January 2003, the rumor mill was working overtime. Between the news shows on the television, which were forecasting (or hoping) for an immediate invasion, and local Marine scuttlebutt, none of the Charlie Battery had any idea of what length of deployment to expect. Phil mentioned to me that he was told to expect an 18-month deployment; LCpl. Warren had heard that it might be as long as 24 months.

Sobering Thoughts

In a move that served to both underscore and highlight the seriousness of this deployment, the Marines Corps issued an order in early January barring Marines from leaving the service. This freeze on discharges was the first since the 1991 Gulf War. It prohibited the approximately 40,000 active service Marines and the Reserves who were scheduled to retire from either leaving the Marine Corps or even changing their military occupational specialty (MOS). But what made it suddenly more realistic and worrisome was when Phil told me the Marine Command was bringing everyone in for an individual meeting, in which they were to sign a last will, arrange allotments, and resolve any personal loose-ends. "I decided that I didn't need to do a last will," he said to me on our last evening together, "because I know I'm coming back."

While this gung-ho attitude was certainly appreciated by anxious parents and spouses, Marine Corps history and tradition certainly indicated that the results could easily be otherwise. With the Marine penchant for studying past battles and campaigns (won and lost) in order to become a more effective fighting force, much time had been spent studying the 19th century British Army as it was deployed around the world in defense of the British Empire.

The British Indian Army of the late 1800s used the expression, "butcher and bolt" to describe their policy of implementing a quick and nasty punitive expedition against troublemaking tribes. The idea behind the policy was not that it was designed to occupy any territory or annex any land, but rather, to use superior firepower and discipline to win quickly—and keep the casualty count to a minimum. While a case might certainly be made to call Saddam Hussein the leader of a "troublemaking tribe," not surprisingly, Marine Corps doctrine followed these "butcher and bolt" tactics. The Marines would go in hard, first and fast; use an overwhelming force; win, and then turn over the peacekeeping and administration to the Army, the United Nations, or some other nominally effective peacekeeping force. But until that happened, as a parent, I hoped Phil was right in his positive prediction of a safe return.

As I drove home in a cold gray January drizzle after saying good-bye to Phil, I was surprisingly calm at the concept of him going off to fight a war. Whether it was from growing up in a Marine Corps family, and my respect and knowledge of his Marine Corps training and tradition, or my complete ignorance of what he was about to encounter—I had no concern that he would be killed or injured. Oddly enough, and at the same time, I was equally at peace with the (absolutely 180-degree opposite) knowledge that if he were killed, there would be a lot of dead Iraqis in front of him, and he would have performed with honor and distinction.

For the first time in my life, I had absolutely no control, influence, or ability to help my son if he needed it. Perhaps in every father's life there comes a time, a day, when you know with absolute clarity and precision that your son has become an adult and left the nest. For me, Saturday, 11 January 2003, was that day, and I felt secure that his training, and that the obstinacy and determination that made him want to join the Marine Corps in the first place, would bring him home safely.

Would I be upset if my son were killed? Words would not describe the depths of my loss. But no one would ever hear it from me, as I had an aggressive, fierce pride in his joining the Marines, and if he joined the Marine gallery of heroes that included 2nd Division, World War II Medal of Honor recipients, such as Alexander Bonneyman and David Shoup, and all the others—what a way for him to be remembered.

Chapter 3

Voyage to Kuwait

Logistics becomes, in fact, the very core of generalship ...
To get military forces into a theatre of war in
superior strength and husband their
strength until they shall prevail.

– S. L. A. Marshall

USS *Ashland*
14 January 2003

Task Force Tarawa—Assault Force East (AF East)—left More-head City, North Carolina, for Kuwait and Iraq on Tuesday, 14 January 2003. AF East boasted three amphibious assault ships: USS *Kearsarge*, USS *Saipan*, and USS *Bataan*; three landing ship docks (LSDs): USS *Ashland*, USS *Gunston Hall*, and USS *Portland*; and the amphibious transport dock (LDP), USS *Ponce*.

USS *Ashland*, a designated LSD, carries both Marines and their gear and is able to land them with or without a pier. Launched in 1988 by Avondale Shipyard in New Orleans, *Ashland* has been upgraded to carry some 400 Marines, as well as a combination of tanks, Humvees, trucks, and other equipment.

This class of ship—along with USS *Ponce*, USS *Portland*, and USS *Gunston Hall*—was designed to accommodate a maximum of four hovercraft. The hovercraft is properly known as a Landing Craft Air Cushioned (LCAC) and carries a combination of Marines, equipment, and vehicles directly from the ship's stern onto any beach the Marines require. The stern of *Ashland* opens out-ward, and each LCAC—powered by four giant fans (two for lift, two for propulsion)—shoots out from the well deck filled with

USS *Ashland*

Marines and their vehicles ready to storm the beach. Since *Ashland* was loading off a normal pier and could be unloaded in Kuwait the same way, she carried two LCACs, and filled the remaining space with 7-ton trucks, M1 Abrams tanks, light armored vehicles (LAVs), water buffalos (300-gallon wheeled water containers), and the other equipment necessary for a long deployment. Most of the heavy armored vehicles were not loaded at Morehead City, but a few days later off the Camp Lejeune coast.

In normal military fashion, Charlie Battery was packed, loaded, and waiting at 0500 on Saturday, 11 January. There they sat and waited, as Phil recalled with disgust, "We hung around the gun park with our gear and our vehicles, until about 1600. I don't know if I was nervous or bored, probably both." Finally, their convoy was released, and about 90 minutes later, they arrived at the piers in Morehead City. "It didn't get any more exciting then," Phil told me later. "Barr and I stood guard duty for the next three days. Four hours on; eight hours off, and we watched the other Marines load the ship. It was cold. It was rainy. It was a crummy assignment. We had our M16s and orders to use them if necessary."

On Tuesday, 14 January, *Ashland* pulled away from the Morehead City pier, and joined the other ships of the convoy. Instead of heading for the North Atlantic, however, she sailed back to Camp Lejeune, and sat off Onslow Beach. At Onslow, the Marines loaded their vehicles into the big LCACs, and then up and into *Ashland*. They brought their howitzers, along with 2nd Marine Division M1 Abrams tanks, Humvees, 7-ton trucks, radars, and LAVs directly from the beach up into the ship. Only then, after getting their equipment loaded and secured, did they head for open water, and the voyage to Kuwait.

Letter from Phil:

17 January 2003

What's going on, Dad?

This has been an interesting couple of days. The chow hall is 24 hours, so we eat and sleep, wake up, and eat again. We play cards and wander around the ship. On Tuesday, we anchored four miles off Onslow Beach and brought tanks on board with hovercrafts. That was cool. Oh yeah, the boat has two gatling guns that fire .50 cal. depleted uranium rounds. They're awesome. Not much else to say, so I'll talk to you later.

Gatling gun aboard USS *Ashland*

In all, Task Force Tarawa left Camp Lejeune and the East Coast for Kuwait and Iraq with the 18 M198 155mm howitzers of the 1/10; 46 amphibious assault vehicles; 24 light armored vehicles; 81 combat aircraft; 14 tanks; 2 counter battery radar, and 2 NBC "Fox" vehicles.[1] The combination of equipment and men on these seven ships comprised a military capability not assembled in anger since the days of Desert Storm in 1991. The transit time from Morehead City to Kuwait Naval Base was plus-minus 30 days, which gave our Charlie Battery Marines time for classes, the gym, and time to smoke and shoot the breeze—the same as thousands of Marines sailing on convoy ships before them.

The Daily Routine

As *Ashland* and the convoy steamed through the North Atlantic, the Marines adjusted quickly to shipboard routine. While we parents of new Marines had no clue what our sons were doing, the parents of the Marines who'd been on USS *Trenton* knew some of what their boys were experiencing. Paul Czombos, whose son, Michael, had been on *Trenton*, said, "I figured he'd spend some time in the weight room, and a lot more time sleeping and taking classes. I assumed it would be more work than his *Trenton* voyage, and they'd keep him busy."

In actuality, the Marines in Assault Force East spent the first few days familiarizing themselves with their respective ships, settling into shipboard routine, and then focusing on their shipboard training, which was oriented to their probable combat operations. While the general route to Kuwait was common knowledge, for some of the newer Marines, the voyage was quite exciting.

It wasn't as cramped as I expected and wandering around the ship was interesting.

LCpl. Philip Lubin

"We sailed across the Atlantic Ocean," Phil told me on his return, "and then we went through the Straits of Gibraltar into the Mediterranean Sea. On the eastern end, we transited the Suez Canal, the Bab el Mandeb Straits, and then the Straits of Hormuz into the Persian Gulf. The weather didn't bother me, so it was a pretty neat trip."

Corporal Aguila related that "On the first Float, the voyage out was very rough, and I was afraid this one would be even worse, being January and all. It almost was—after only two days—we got caught in a big storm off Bermuda, and we lost two days detouring around it."

After a week, the daily shipboard routine became monotonous. A daily routine was sleeping from 2200 to 0600 (after a few days, the ship did quiet down during these hours) with breakfast from 0600 to 0800, lunch from 1100 to 1300, and dinner from 1600 to 1930. In between, they had classes, played cards, went to the gym, and just hung out.

Ashland had three gyms, and between classes, anyone interested could lift weights and work out. Many did. Aerobics equipment, along with weights, were available, and the gyms had regular hours for the Marines. Several Charlie Battery Marines all worked out regularly. Corporal Czombos said, "What else was there for us to do?" Lance Corporal Turcotte, on the other hand, found the ship's library, and he read regularly and drank coffee. Additionally, the ship had an excellent movie selection. Each room had its own television, with four channels, and there was a twelve-page list of movies from which the Marines could choose. Corporal Noyes laughed as he remembered, "Other than the fact we were going off to war, it really wasn't bad. Weapons training was easy, the chow hall served some pretty good food, and we watched movies the rest of the time!"

Much of their spare time was spent hanging out with their friends, listening to music, and just trying to stay relaxed. "We all brought CDs and CD players," said LCpl. Jones. "Lubin had Metallica, the Chili Peppers, and the Stones. Other guys brought Guns n Roses, Insane Clown Posse, Anthrax, rap; there was a lot of music." There were regular card games, chess games, and the usual BS sessions; in short, *Ashland* was like any other Marine troopship since 1916.

Even though they were on a Navy ship, the Marines still had daily responsibilities beyond classes, working out, sleeping and listening to music. Lance Corporal Turcotte, for example, was tasked with maintaining the security of all the vehicles on the weather deck. After the Marines loaded their vehicles from Onslow Beach, it was essential that someone check the tie-down straps securing the vehicles at least twice daily, to be sure that the constant pitching and rolling from the seas didn't loosen the lines. "I was posted

On *Trenton*, we were rolling 45–50 degrees. A lot of guys were sick. This time, it was much easier.

LCpl. Joseph Turcotte

One day, we named our howitzers. We named ours 'Camel Thumper' because it seemed to be an appropriate name.

LCpl. Philip Lubin

to the Combat Cargo Unit, and basically we had to check our guns to ensure that nothing had worked loose. The seas were actually pretty mild for the North Atlantic in January, but it's still important to be sure our gear is in good order."

Shipboard Training

As a career Marine, and a veteran of both Operation Desert Storm in 1991 and Somalia in 1993, MSgt. Santivasci knew better than most what to expect, and knew in what areas these young Charlie Battery Marines needed reinforcing. He had training in both individual survival measures, as well as unit-level training. They also trained them—again and again—in changing contaminated Mission-Oriented Protective Posture (MOPP) gear, in crew-served weapons, land navigation, first aid, basic Arabic phrases, Call-For-Fire missions, how to handle enemy prisoners of war, along with combat rules of engagement. And even though MSgt. Santivasci was on USS *Gunston Hall* teaching classes to those Marines, he knew that 1st Lt. Shea and GySgt. Lambert had been in combat during Operation Desert Storm, so he was confident that they'd have Charlie Battery pumped up and trained by the time they arrived in Kuwait. This knowledge, added to his normal responsibilities, let him know what he needed to accomplish on shipboard before they arrived in Kuwait.

In addition, on the way over, 1st Lt. Shea conducted personal, but informal interviews with every Marine in his Guns platoon. "I made sure I had all the next-of-kin information, that they were aware of what was going on, and they understood they were ready; even if they felt they were not. Other than that, it was a matter of taking care of staff work and preparing for combat operations by overseeing classes." Regardless of their rank, responsibility, or area of specialty, shipboard training was the major part of every Marine's daily routine.

Nuclear, Biological, Chemical (NBC) Training

Doc Sanders explained his role in detail, "We spent a lot of time learning about possible Iraqi NBC weapons, and their antidotes. We studied nerve agents like Sarin, Tabun, and VX, along with blood agents and the old-style poison gasses like mustard gas." He needed to educate his Marines on how to react to the various chemical weapons. Nerve agents, or other gasses like chlorine, for example, are denser than air, and will collect in low-lying areas like the fighting pits. So the Marines had to be aware of that, as well as how to use the antidotes that were available to them. As a result, the Marines spent a lot of time practicing the antidote training, where they had to give a buddy a shot through his MOPP suit, or through his cammis. These classes were no place to screw around, and Sanders made sure they took the NBC training very seriously.

Lance Corporal Lamb added that he probably had more NBC training than anyone else in Charlie Battery, except for Sanders. In addition to the normal Marine NBC training, Lamb took the Enhanced NBC School course, which educates a person on how to live and fight in an NBC environment. He also had the special training on how to read and use the NBC detectors. "It's pretty involved; if you don't practice it daily, it's easy to lose the technique, so we practiced with the equipment every day." All Marines were issued MOPP suits, and they completed intensive training in them on board ship as well. MOPPs are the protective gear soldiers wear to protect themselves in case of an NBC attack. The pants are bulky, because they're lined with carbon, sort of like the fish filter in an aquarium. The shirt has a hood, and of course, the gas masks, which hang from theirs belts, always within arm's reach.

> We spent a lot of time learning about possible Iraqi NBC weapons, and their antidotes.
>
> *Doc Sanders*

> These classes had a sense of urgency. This time it was going to be for real.
>
> *Cpl. Chris Gault*

Crew-Served Weapons Training

Corporal Czombos, who always liked to shoot, remembered the classes in crew-served weapons. "We broke down the Mark19 Automatic Grenade launcher, the M249 SAW, which is a beefed-up 16, as well as the M240 Golf, and the .50 cal. machine gun. These are great weapons, and I was certainly ready to use any one of them!"

Even though this artillery battery's main weapon is the M198 155mm howitzer, the old adage, "Every Marine, a rifleman," still holds true. Like every Marine, Phil knows the weapon details inside-out. His own personal weapon is an M16, a gas-fired rifle with a cyclic firing rate of 800 rounds per minute. He can break it down and clean it in the dark or blindfolded. "Every Marine can do that. We learn how to use our rifle from the first days of boot camp, and then practice with it constantly."

Other crew-served weapons the Charlie Battery Marines are trained to operate and fire include the Mark19, which fires a belt of 48 rifle grenades and has a cyclic firing rate of 375 to 425 rounds per minute. Then they have the M249, which fires a .223 round off a 200-round belt at 1,000 rounds per minute. Their M240 Golf replaced the older M60 automatic rifle, which had replaced the older BAR. The 240 fires a 7.62mm caliber round at a rate of 650 to 950 rounds per minute, and it weighs 21 pounds loaded in comparison to 21 pounds unloaded for the M60.

Lance Corporal Souza thought the classes were helpful, as some Marines needed more training than others. He recalls they attended weapons classes every single day in addition to battlefield first aid classes and NBC classes. "Some of the new guys didn't seem to get it, so we helped them after the official class was done. We handle this sort of stuff—the slower guys—ourselves. Marines are all on the same team."

> **We emphasized this was for real, and they sat up and paid attention, especially to the battlefield first-aid and NBC classes.**
>
> *SSgt. John Fontenoy*

Corporal Gallagher remembered how officers instructed classes in everything they thought Marines might encounter in Iraq. They had classes on what to do with unexploded ordinance, in land mines, in NBC attacks, in NBC-infected battlefields, in battlefield first-aid, and of course, being an artillery battery, in basic artillery schooling. "If they had an idea to keep me alive, I certainly listened." In addition to the classes, the Marines were able to have some live-fire exercises to break the daily monotony of shipboard life. Corporal Aguila recalled how one time they were allowed to sight-in and fire their M16s from the helicopter deck. They set up some targets off the stern, and soldiers tried to catch the rhythm of the ship's pitch and roll as they fired. "We were pretty awful, but it was a lot of fun."

Cultural Insights

The Marines did not simply focus on weapons and NBC training; in fact, the classes varied in content from the military to the cultural. While the Marines all studied and restudied their weapons systems, tactics, and strategy, many of the Charlie Battery Marines found the other classes equally interesting. Even though most of Charlie Battery had been to Djibouti, a small country on the Horn of Africa and off the tip of Somalia, this operation into the Persian Gulf was the first any of them would spend any significant time in-country. Lance Corporal Bechu said, "The Marine Corps wanted to teach us how not to piss people off on purpose."

In one of his classes, the Marines informed them not to worry about guys walking around holding hands, "because Arab men were friendly, and not queer." They were told not to show the soles of their feet to others, not to use their left hand to eat, and to not give anyone a thumbs-up sign. These common gestures that were fine for Americans were offensive to Iraqis.

Rules of Engagement (ROE) Classes

Classes were taught with the utmost seriousness. The ROE classes concerned most of the Marines who were going off to war for the first time. The ROEs are a code of conduct, or a set of guidelines, which are effectively more accurately known as the rules of war. The Marine Corps was adamant that every Marine know what to do in a given situation. "There were a lot of rules on how we were to conduct ourselves with the Iraqis, both soldiers and civilians," said Cpl. Delarosa.

The Marines knew enough not to shoot unarmed civilians, but officers gave the Marines many scenarios as to whether they should shoot or not. One scenario they used was regarding the Red Crescent, which is the Iraqis' version of the American Red Cross. They were told to stay alert for (and not shoot) ambulances with a Red Crescent on them. Other scenarios were more serious and difficult to determine. Corporal Hebert had the same concerns as his fellow Marines. "My worry was how they'd match up to what I thought we might encounter in a real war situation. Basically, every Iraqi with a weapon was to be considered an enemy, and should be killed. That's fine for the men, but I was worried about how we'd decide about their women and children. Being an arty battery, I assumed we wouldn't have to worry about this kind of stuff; that the infantry had to worry about these situations more than us."

Phil was more relaxed about the ROEs and said that while he wasn't any kind of expert, he felt most of the scenarios could be dealt with using common sense. "You don't normally shoot women and children, but someone with a weapon is fair game. I figured I'd work it out as we went along."

Spiritual Guidance

In addition to learning about the morality and details of fighting a war, the Marine Corps provided its troops with both material and

---

CFLCC ROE CARD

1. On order, enemy military and paramilitary forces are declared hostile and may be attacked subject to the following instructions:

   a. Positive Identification (PID) is required prior to engagement. PID is a reasonable certainty that the proposed target is a legitimate military target. If no PID, contact your next higher commander for decision.

   b. Do not engage anyone who has surrendered or is out of battle due to sickness or wounds.

   c. Do not target or strike any of the following except in self-defense to protect yourself, your unit, friendly forces, and designated persons or property under your control:
   - Civilians
   - Hospitals, mosques, churches, shrines, schools, museums, national monuments, and any other historical and cultural sites

   d. Do not fire into civilian populated areas or buildings unless the enemy is using them for military purposes or if necessary for your self-defense. Minimize collateral damage.

   e. Do not target enemy Infrastructure (public works, commercial communication facilities, dams), Lines of Communication (roads, highways, tunnels, bridges, railways) and Economic Objects (commercial storage facilities, pipelines) unless necessary for self-defense or if ordered by your commander. If you must fire on these objects to engage a hostile force, disable and disrupt but avoid destruction of these objects, if possible.

ROE Card – front

They taught us how to deal with civilians and how to deal with any EPWs (enemy prisoners of war) we would capture.

Cpl. Gaspar Aguila

CFLCC ROE CARD

2. The use of force, including deadly force, is authorized to protect the following:

- Yourself, your unit, and friendly forces
- Enemy Prisoners of War
- Civilians from crimes that are likely to cause death or serious bodily harm, such as murder or rape
- Designated civilians and/or property, such as personnel of the Red Cross/Crescent, UN, and US/UN supported organizations.

3. Treat all civilians and their property with respect and dignity. Do not seize civilian property, including vehicles, unless you have the permission of a company level commander and you give a receipt to the property's owner.

4. Detain civilians if they interfere with mission accomplishment or if required for self-defense.

5. CENTCOM General Order No. 1A remains in effect. Looting and the taking of war trophies are prohibited.

REMEMBER

- Attack enemy forces and military targets.
- Spare civilians and civilian property, if possible.
- Conduct yourself with dignity and honor.
- Comply with the Law of War. If you see a violation, report it.

These ROE will remain in effect until your commander orders you to transition to post-hostilities ROE.

AS OF 311330Z JAN 03

ROE Card – back

spiritual needs, regardless of rank, time, or grade. "I shipped out on the Bataan," said Chaps Ritchie, "and I had over 1,000 Marines on board to whom I needed to minister. We're a dynamic ministry; we live with the Marines—we go where they go, and do what they do, so I was constantly busy. Most of these Marines had never fought, so I had a lot of one-on-one conversations, along with small group talks, on the voyage over."

Comparing This Voyage to the Trenton Float

This voyage to Kuwait was different than Charlie Battery's previous float on USS *Trenton* in 2002 because this time they were sure they were heading towards war. Although a float is conducted on virtually a war footing, there was an edge, and an urgency, to their training that had been missing from their first time in the Persian Gulf.

On the *Trenton* float, USS *Trenton* had stopped in Djibouti and Oman for desert training, and then later moored off Pakistan in order to drop off various Special Forces groups who were headed up to Afghanistan. They had departed soon after 9/11, and the Marines of Charlie Battery thought that they would be off-loaded and fighting the Taliban someplace. There was a lot of disappointment when they weren't.

On 9/11, the Charlie Battery Marines were at Fort Bragg, North Carolina, training on their howitzers. As the news of the terror attack spread through the United States, suddenly, Fort Bragg was placed on full alert. Tanks rolled up to the front gate and infantry with loaded rifles were stationed alongside the tanks. The field op (operation) was cancelled, and they hustled Charlie Battery back to Camp Lejeune. "We were so ready to go fight," Corporal Czombos said. "We should have gone end-to-end in that stupid part of the world, and just cleaned it the fuck up." However, the Bush administration and the Marine Corps had other plans, and Charlie Battery and the other Marines on the Trenton were tasked as a Marine Expeditionary Unit (MEU), which meant they acted as a rapid response force, with port calls to various Persian Gulf locations for specialized training.

While on the *Trenton* float, they trained in Djibouti, which was hot and miserable. Corporal Goodson was less than complimentary about the desert environment and its inhabitants. "We did security training; how to secure an airfield and all, and we did some live-fire exercises. It wasn't even an attractive desert; just coarse sand and some scruff. The local people were so poor; it was pathetic to see them. We gave them food and water; they were thankful for whatever we gave them. The kids would steal and eat our garbage, so I can't imagine what they normally ate. I tried some of local food, chicken and rice; it was pretty wretched."

After they left Djibouti, they spent 107 straight days in the Persian Gulf on board *Trenton*, a Marine float record for not stopping in a port. Corporal Gault related how "It was horrible. They tried to keep us busy with classes, but after a few weeks, everyone realized we were just marking time."

Port of Call: Belleau Wood in France

After *Trenton* left the Persian Gulf, they had a liberty in the Seychelles, and then had a port call in France on the voyage home. Most of the Marines took the train to Paris, which they enjoyed, and then many of them took a special tour of the battlefield at Belleau Wood. It was at their tour of the Belleau Wood battlefield where several of the Charlie Battery Marines began to understand the mystique that surrounds the Marine Corps, and what makes Marines so different than any other branch of the service.

Belleau Wood was the first battle that the Americans fought during World War I, as well as the first time the Marines fought under their own, and not Army, command. With the Allied armies having been bled white during the previous four years of trench warfare, it was at Belleau Wood that the Marines answered the world's questions of Would the Americans fight? Can they win? Who are these Marines?

The Marines answered all these questions at "The Wood," fighting with a ferocity that earned them the name "Devildogs" from the German veterans they defeated, as well as honors from Great Britain's Royal Marines. Royal Marine Gen. David Meyer cabled after their stunning victory and declared his "heartiest congratulations ... and may the future bring us closer together."[1] (Nearly 90 years later, little did the Charlie Battery Marines realize just how close they would become with the Royal Marines.) Even the French Army they saved recognized them, belatedly, as they renamed the woods, and declared *"Bois de Belleau* shall be named *'Bois de la Brigade de Marine.'"*[2]

The wheat field near Belleau Wood, France

Most important for the men of Charlie Battery was how they began to see and understand the Marine Corps history they studied in boot camp and afterwards, and how Marine Corps tradition basically started right there, in The Wood. "We looked across the wheat field," LCpl. Jones said, "where the Marines walked through a half-mile of German machine gun fire. This is where Dan Daily jumped up, and shouted, 'Come on, you sons of bitches! Do you want to live forever?' We had learned all this in boot camp, and it was a sobering experience to actually be where it happened."

Upon visiting the The Wood's wheatfield, LCpl. Turcotte reflected on whether or not he could do what those WWI Marines had done. He pondered if he "could measure up to their standards." It was probably this mindset, with these Charlie Battery Marines wondering vaguely if they could 'measure up' that led them to join the Corps, and it was this same mindset, but with two years of Marine Corps training behind them, that had them prepared for war by the time they deployed on USS *Ashland*.

Amphibious Task Force East in the Red Sea

Near the Voyage's End

For many of the Marines, one of the highlights of the voyage was when they were able to see the 2003 SuperBowl. While Tampa Bay stomped Oakland, the Marines of Charlie Battery and Task Force Tarawa were sailing through the eastern end of the Mediterranean Sea, as they neared their destination.

Letter from Phil:

25 January 2003

What's going on, Dad?

Right now, we are around six days from the Suez Canal. It's been pretty cool; they helo supplies on to us every day. I've been getting some great pictures. There is a TV on board so we get to see the news and movies and TV shows every day. We got our smallpox shots today. Oh yeah, when we go through the Suez and the Straits of Gibraltar and other places like that, I'm going to be manning a .50 cal for boat security because the canal is so narrow. No one is allowed outside when we go, but I will, so I'll get some awesome pics. I got some pictures of the Kearsarge sailing next to us. It's the lead ship. Not much else to say, so I'll write later.

For all but Phil, and two other Charlie Battery Marines, the voyage was a repeat of their *Trenton* float. Across the Atlantic, through the Straits of Gibraltar, then steaming east through the

Southern entrance of the Suez Canal

Mediterranean Sea, and down through the Suez Canal. For the new Marines, though, it was quite a sight-seeing experience, as Phil said, "I went on deck a lot. This was my first time at sea, and to be doing this, and also see the other ships in the convoy, struck me as pretty neat. I brought a lot of disposable cameras, and I got a lot of pictures."

Letter from Phil:

7 February 2003

What's going on, Dad?

I'm on a .50 cal. when we go through the canals, and when we went through the Suez, I got great pictures of Egypt. I got one of me giving the finger to a mosque with the Egyptian Army in front. Today we're going through the Straits of Hormuz into the Persian Gulf. It should be cool. We're getting off in Kuwait in like six days, After that, who knows. It's in the 90s here with humidity, so it's real nice. I've got to go so I'll talk to you then.

When not playing "diplomat" for the Marine Corps, Phil and the other Marines, spent time on deck looking at the variety of ships and scenery in the Suez Canal as they made the transit.

When going thru the Suez Canal, security was tight. Corporal Noyes added, "I was on the re-act team. We were stationed mid-ship,

Security station in the Red Sea

with our M16s at the ready, in case we were ordered to move to wherever we might be needed if we were actually attacked. I didn't really see much chance that some Arab might make it past the Cobras' tanks, Humvees, and Lubin's .50."

It took 30 days for the men and ships of Assault Force East to arrive in Kuwait. On 15 February, *Ashland* unloaded the Marines and their cargo via her LCACs onto Blue Beach One, a section of the Kuwaiti coast secured by the Kuwait Naval Base. "Unless you were a driver, you just watched," said LCpl. Turcotte. "I guessed that the easy time was over," Phil added. "I had no clue what was going to happen next, so I figured I'd just listen up and do my best."

None of the parents, wives, or girlfriends had any clue what was happening. I'd received only one letter at this point, written when Phil was loading equipment off of Onslow Beach back in mid-January. A dozen times a day, I would look at my world atlas, usually the section on the Mediterranean Sea and the Persian Gulf, and wonder where my son was and how he was faring.

As we made the crossing through the Suez, I could see Humvees and tanks running along side of us, and there were Cobra helicopters flying cover over us all.

LCpl. Phil Lubin

Get up, boys, get up and go. That's the quickest way to get it over.

Lt. Col. Lewis B. Puller
on the Inchon-Seoul highway
September 1950

Chapter 4

Camp Shoup

So do not fear, for I am with you;
Do not be dismayed,
For I am your God.
I will strengthen you and help you.

Isaiah 41:10

*As quoted by Chaplain Ritchie when
talking with the Marines at Camp Shoup*

**Kuwaiti Desert
17 February–19 March 2003**

Camp Shoup, located some 30 miles from the Iraqi border, existed only as a grid on a map of the Kuwaiti desert before Task Force Tarawa's mid-February arrival. The Kuwaiti desert is desolate. Unlike Iraq, which has the Tigris and Euphrates rivers irrigating the country and leaving strands of greenery along their banks, once you leave the Kuwaiti seacoast, there is nothing but bland and coarse sand, along with a constantly blowing wind. The only man-made structures visible are the power lines that shimmer hazily in the heat before blending into the horizon. In short, Camp Shoup was in the middle of nothing. Before the Marines arrived, the only movement came from the occasional camel trains, as the Bedouins herded their animals south to Kuwait City. But between the efforts of local Kuwaiti contractors and the Marines, this barren piece of desert was quickly transformed into a fully functional Marine base.

Unlike the Army bases—which our televisions revealed had basketball courts, served Kentucky Fried Chicken, and offered computer cafes, email access, air-conditioned tents, movies, and shoppettes—Camp Shoup existed only to give the Marines of Task Force Tarawa and Charlie Battery a staging area for their probable attack into Iraq.

The 2nd Marine Expeditionary Brigade (MEB) discharged 2,800 Marines and vehicle loads via each vessel's LCACs onto the Kuwaiti shore in only two and one-half days, and then began to move the men and equipment upcountry into their camps. The remaining equipment, primarily ammunition, was unloaded in the next two and one-half days, and transported to its respective depots. "They unloaded everything we had a day quicker than we loaded it back in the States," Phil said. "Those guys really worked. Then it was our turn to go."

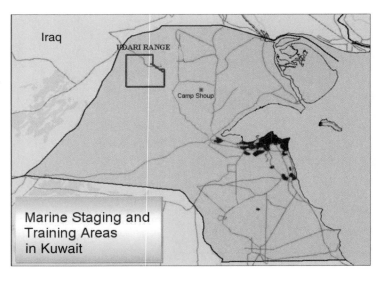

Marine Staging and Training Areas in Kuwait

Phil, LCpl. Bechu, and their section chief, Cpl. Wilson, were in the first small group of Marines who left early to help establish the camp. Known as the advance party (AP), they departed immediately from Kuwait Naval Base for Camp Shoup. Phil and Bechu sat in the back of the 7-ton for three hours and watched their gun. They were on Tube Watch, which meant the barrel of the gun was locked down, and it was their job to see the rough roads didn't jar it loose. The remaining members of Charlie Battery, as well as the other Marines of Task Force Tarawa, were bussed to the camp the next day. Their trip, with an Army driver, was far different than that of Phil, Bechu, and Wilson's.

> Once we left the port, Kuwait was ugly. Just sand and dust, and the wind never stopped blowing.
>
> *LCpl. Sobola Bechu*

Passing a camel train on the way to Camp Shoup

Camp Shoup's protective berm

Lance Corporal Turcotte related how they were all bussed up to the camp, which is fairly close to the Iraqi border, on a major highway. Camp Shoup was maybe ten miles off the highway, but the Army driver got lost. What should have been a 2- or 3-hour drive took them 13 hours. "This guy was a total asshole; he was completely ignorant and unprepared. And that was the best part of the day!" When they finally arrived, Camp Shoup was no bargain. "To be charitable, the camp was an impromptu affair, just rows and rows of large green general purpose (GP) tents."

As this point, I still had not received any mail from Phil. He'd been gone approximately five weeks, and I had no clue where he was, or what he was encountering. Then one day, I received a newsletter from the commanding officer of 1/10, which had been sent to every parent and spouse.

Newsletter from Lt. Col. Glenn Starnes:

19 February 2003

Life in Camp Shoup is not great, but it could be worse. All of RCT-2 is housed in this camp. We are surrounded by a ten-foot high berm of sand. The camp itself is flat desert. Everyone is housed in 18-man tents ... while these tents do not have floors, they do provide protection from the elements that include: a constant wind, blowing dust and sand ....

Camp Life: "What A Mess!"

Later, Cpl. Aguila added a few comments to Col. Starnes' letter. "I heard that Shoup was one of the most primitive of the camps, but hey, since we're not the Army, we didn't expect much better. But they could have fixed up the camp more; we didn't have electricity, toilets, or water. We lived on MREs and bottled water for the first two weeks." Ever polite, LCpl. Bechu tried to put a nice spin on the camp by saying "Being AP, we brought up the guns before the main force arrived. The camp was a mess. I'd been in Djibouti, on our *Trenton* float, but this seemed worse. It was very confused."

There weren't many kinds words for the Army contractors and planners either. Despite the month-long voyage to Kuwait, the camp was still being built when the troops arrived. Contractors were still pushing up berms around the tents.

Camp life did not get any more enjoyable as that first week passed, and with no shower facilities, people started smelling ripe. Lance Corporal Turcotte grimaced as he remembered "even though we all smelled the same, it was really pretty awful." Corporal Czombos added, "We were all wearing our MOPPs 24/7, so after a couple of weeks, we were nasty!" Adding to the discomfort, Phil recalled, with a laugh, how "the MREs get you all bound up, so all you do is fart like crazy. And our MOPP pants were pulled tight, so you had like two weeks of farts stored up in your pants. It was a good thing we were out in the desert!"

The sleeping conditions were particularly unattractive. Marines slept on the sand in their sleeping bags. Since the tents had no flooring, they tried to remove the biggest rocks and lumps, and simply threw their sleeping bags down on the sand. With 17 to 20 gassy, smelly men to a tent, no electricity, no running water, an outdoor field shower perhaps once every five days, several wondered why they didn't try to sleep outside.

Lieutenant Colonel Starnes' monthly newsletter from February continued and confirmed the unfavorable picture of Camp Shoup life, although he did so in a somewhat more polite, parent-friendly manner:

Newsletter from Lt. Col. Glenn Starnes:

Chris Gault "enjoying" an MRE

I was surprised how cold it got at night. My idea of the Middle East and the desert is that it was sandy and hot.

LCpl. Philip Lubin

We were all wearing our MOPPs 24/7, so after a couple of weeks, we were nasty!

Cpl. Michael Czombos

Head call

I'm from Zaire, and I left during the civil war. I lived in some terrible places, but at least in Zaire, I understood why the camps were so ugly.

LCpl. Sobola Bechu

19 February 2003

... Bottled water and MREs are delivered daily. We hope to have hot chow two times a day beginning soon. A large number of portable toilets have been positioned throughout the camp. We are also promised portable showers in the next few days ....

For bathrooms, the Marines had outdoor latrines. Basically, the Kuwaiti contractors trucked in Port-O-Jons. If you think a line of Port-O-Jons smells bad after two days at a soccer tournament, imagine approximately 7,000 men in the desert using the same heads that are cleaned approximately weekly. Many had no roofs, and most were filled to overflowing.

All of this might have been more bearable had the food situation been better. After two weeks, the MREs gave way to hot meals that were dished up in the mess tents, which were the same simple GP tents, similar to what the Marines slept it, and were no match for the flies and dust. The tents were clogged with sand, and dust settled everywhere. With flickering fluorescent lighting shining down on cheap, plastic plates, and hordes of flies competing with Marines for the food, chow time was necessary, but miserable. Most agreed the flies were worse than the sand. Many recall having to eat with one hand, while waving the flies off with the other, often, scraping the flies off the food they were trying to eat.

The only luxuries or recreational items available in Camp Shoup were those brought to the camp by the individual Marines. Such luxuries included CD players, decks of cards, and various smutty magazines. Between the voyage over on *Ashland*, and the time in Camp Shoup, many young Marines said they'd read more *Sports Illustrated*s, *Maxim*s, *Playboy*s, and *Newsweek*s than ever.

Relaxing in the tent

Camp Shoup was a true battle camp. Only a few embedded reporters braved the camp's setting, and no cameras from CNN, MSNBC, or Fox marched in to broadcast stories of these Marines back to America. Camp Shoup's rough and grim lifestyle would do very little to attract new recruits back home. Rather, the camp existed for one reason only—to house the 7,000 Marines of Task Force Tarawa as they prepared and trained for war. In fact, within a week of arriving, Charlie Battery and their battalion moved into the field for their first field operation.

> **In Shoup, what we ate and how we ate was just gross.**
>
> *LCpl. Philip Lubin*

Udairi Training Range

Phil, the rest of Charlie Battery, and the other Marines of 1/10 moved out to the Udairi Training Range on February 20 in order to train and prepare for the expected lengthy combat operations. The Udairi Range was located in western Kuwait, some 30 miles from Camp Shoup, and gave most of the Marines an eye-opening experience in desert warfare. The Kuwaiti government built the Udairi Training Range after Operation Desert Storm to provide a live-fire training area for the Coalition Forces. Located in northwest Kuwait, some 15 miles from the Iraqi border, the training range provided the Marines (and other Coalition soldiers) an opportunity to calibrate and fire their weapons after the long sea-voyage from the United States. Equally important was its immense size (approximately 180 square miles), which enabled the Marines to practice their combined armor—artillery—mechanized infantry and close air support, as well as acclimate the Marines to the vagaries of the February–March winter weather in Kuwait, which

Firing practice on the Udairi Training Range

Goodson, Barr, and Aguila in front of the lead Humvee

was far worse than what most of Charlie Battery had experienced in Djibouti while on the *Trenton* float.

The Kuwaiti desert's winter environment is always cold, and if it doesn't rain, sandstorms prevail. Troops had to wear goggles all the time, but when the storms intensified, visibility went to barely above zero. There were days when they endured severe sandstorms with winds over 50 mph. "A lot of the time the temperature was in the 40s," LCpl. Turcotte complained. "It was cold and damp, and the winds seemed to blow constantly. I think I had sand in every possible body part."

That first field op lasted eight days and got them all back into shape quickly. Round-the-clock operations included live-fire training with their 155mms, along with battery defense, and crew-served weapons practice. Officers drilled them hard, but they were a lot sharper on the way back from Udairi than when they got there. Our Charlie Battery Marines picked up their training with a greater intensity than they had expected. There was an urgency and a nastiness that the senior NCOs worked to instill in their young Marines. Corporal Gault related how the attitude had changed at the Udairi Training Range. "We worked harder than we'd worked for a long time. We practiced for speed and accuracy, over and over. Gunny had trained us hard back home, but he had an attitude about training that we'd never seen before." Instead of sand berms, Corporal Hebert remembers stacking sandbags inside their 7-ton trucks for protection against incoming Iraqi fire.

> I needed them to be able to think on their own. I yelled a little and cursed a little, and they caught on real quickly.
>
> *Gunny Lambert*

"Camp Shoup was about gun maintenance and live fire exercises. Charlie Battery is an artillery battery; this is what we are all about," explains 1st Lt. Shea. So, the coordination on a howitzer battery, be it Charlie, Bravo, or any other, is of utmost importance. While the ballet of loading and firing the howitzer (like Phil and the crew on Gun #1) is what leads to speed and accuracy, it is the coordination between the entire battery (fire direction control and the gun crews), as well as how and where the gun is sited, that make for a successful mission. The advance party (AP) is responsible for finding the best place to site their guns. This was an integral part of the mission, as Top Santivasci explained the role of the ground guides:

> One or two Marines from every howitzer section will be ordered to go forward whenever we received an order to move. They move up in the Humvee to the ordered area, perform a security sweep, and then find the actual place to best site the gun. They set the azimuth for when the gun is laid, as well as find the best route off the road to get to where they want to put the gun.

Desert "Wildlife"

During their week in the field, the living conditions at Camp Shoup had not improved. In fact, with the arrival of the Marines, and their food, warmth, and refuse, the local bug and insect populations had migrated to the camp.

Upon returning from their first field operation, Charlie Battery concentrated on equipment maintenance and hygiene. With the conditions in Camp Shoup remaining so primitive, it was essential that each Marine be as cognizant of the potential health hazards as possible. This was a difficult assignment, however, as the desert wildlife, a varied selection of bugs and insects, far outnumbered the Marines in the camp. All the Charlie Battery Marines remembered the sand flies and the beetles. Corporal Hebert recalled that "the flies would come at you in waves. You would have to swat your way through clouds of them. It was just disgusting."

Adding to the overwhelming fly population, the Marines were quickly introduced to a local desert beetle known as the dung beetle. Appropriately named for its choice of food, the beetles congregated by the latrines. Lance Corporal Warren recalled them with disgust. "You'd be sitting in the head and you'd hear this rustling or soft scratching sound. That was the stupid beetles, moving through the sand to the heads."

If the dung beetles weren't enough to liven the camp up, the Marines could count on scarabs as well—those big, round, black beetles made famous by the recent movie, "The Mummy." Phil told me how the scarabs would burrow up from the sand. "You'd

It was like a plague you read about in the Bible. Texas has bugs, but this was amazing!

Cpl. Geoffrey Goodson

Tent pet

You don't understand how big and nasty these spiders are!

LCpl. Philip Lubin

The camel-killer spider

be standing there, and they'd just pop up from underneath your boot. They were as big around as your fist, and had a hard shell." Corporal Czombos, however, saw some humor in these giant beetles and recounted how one day, Phil, who was not particularly fond of the beetles, finally got "grossed out" one too many times and started whacking one big beetle with LCpl. Turcotte's sledgehammer. "It just exploded, and he had all this black beetle shit over his pants and shirt, and he kept beating the pieces and yelling at it. It was great to watch!"

Not to be outdone by a scarab, scorpions played a role in plaguing the young men as well. When asked about the desert wildlife, Cpl. Hebert admitted to a painful encounter with a black scorpion. He recalled how one night, he got stung three times by the same black scorpion who was trapped in his sleeping bag. "It hurt like hell, and it gave me a big-ass blister on my left ass cheek!" Cpl. Aguila laughed and said, "It was the size of a golf ball!"

Scorpions weren't the only odd bedfellows the Marines had to battle. The desert lizards—which were much larger than scorpions—often found their way into tents and competed with Marines for sleeping space.

Last, but not least, there were the desert spiders dubbed "camel killers." These very large, hairy, poisonous beasts prompted some forms of entertainment among the Marines. For some, flicking the spiders at others when they weren't looking created a diversion from daily camp life. Others had more colorful experiences with the camel killers, including LCpl. Turcotte and my son, Phil. Ever inquisitive, as well as being bored beyond belief, Turcotte played with the local wildlife. "The camel killers were nasty. They'd try to hide behind the tires and other gear, but they were so big, we'd see them anyway. One day, I was poking one with a stick, and it bit the stick, and I was able to pick it up, like a hooked fish. This thing just didn't let go!" Phil remembered the spiders too. He recalls, "The best part about the spiders was when you threw them in the fire, you could hear them shrieking. They were loud!"

Letter from Phil:

27 February 2003

What's up, Dad?

I hate Kuwait. It's just a big desert with lots of stinky little Arabs. We just got back from an eight-day field op. It was cold and there were sandstorms every day. Fun. We were supposed to go to Iraq in three days, but that was cancelled. Now we don't know, but we should be in North Carolina by July 15. Who knows? I'm writing this in my gas mask because we're doing NBC training today. What's new with you? I don't really have a lot to write because all the stuff I want to tell you I don't want to write, I'd rather tell you. Talk to you later.

A General's Visit

A few days later, on 1 March, Camp Shoup's Marines received a visit from Lt. Gen. James Conway, the commanding general of the 1st Marine Expeditionary Force (MEF). He came to inspire his Marines concerning their probable invasion of Iraq. Standing atop a tank, he drew cheers from the Marines as he told them that most of the United States was in favor of military action, but he drew more applause as he went on to tell them that the Marines who fought in Desert Storm left two legacies for them to live up to: "First of all, all of Iraq knows we are the baddest mother-fuckers in the valley . . . and second, they know we have the largest air combat wing in the whole Marine Corps for us to use."

Right at that point, two F18s came screaming in from the desert, right overhead, right on the deck. "Just fucking awesome," Cpl. Czombos nodded as he remembered the fighter display. He added how two Cobras hovered overhead, doing figure-8s. "I was so anxious to go get some Iraqis." Phil recalled how the fighter jets were so low, he could see their missile loads, and one guy who had his gatling gun swiveling back and forth. It was a show to get the Marines fired up and ready to go. And it worked for Cpl. Hebert, who admitted, "It got me really wired up. I'd signed up to defend my country, and this was going to be my chance."

Lieutenant General Conway finished his visit by saying, "How you conduct yourselves here, what you do here, will govern how you, your compadres, and your family sees you for the rest of your lives …. Go out there and do what you need to do." [3] After the general's departure, they all took a run around the perimeter of Camp Shoup; just another way the Marine Corps kept their warriors toned and fit, yet under control.

Waiting to Invade

As Lt. Gen. Conway and his officers worked on getting their Marines physically and emotionally ready for battle, Chaps Ritchie and his fellow chaplains—1/10's Lt. Kevin Norton, 1/2's Father (LT, USN) Dan Hoedl, and 3/2's Chaplain Brian Waite—continued to work on their Marines' spiritual needs. "We offered a nondenominational service, which was very popular," Ritchie said. "We had a Catholic priest, as well as several Protestant ministers, and we'd do these big joint services. And we would just walk through the camp, and the Marines would be calling out 'Hey, chaplain, over here.' For all their rough-and-tough, macho Marine attitudes, they're still a bunch of very worried kids." For these young Marines, a chaplain represents God's presence, and Chaplain Ritchie, Father Hoedl, and Chaplain Waite represented that presence in Camp Shoup.

What Lt. Gen. Conway did not tell his Marines that day at Camp Shoup was that they were taking part in the most involved land mission in Marine history. Task Force Tarawa, under the control of Conway's 1st MEF, consisted of infantry, tanks, LAVs, artillery, and amphibious assault vehicles, along with support of the 3rd Marine Air Wing. In fact, for the first time in the history of Army-Marine joint military campaigns, there were more Marines involved in Operation Iraqi Freedom than soldiers. Whether this was due to the unusual war plan that emphasized speed and adaptability, or simply the Marine Corps' amazing ability to recall and successfully deploy some 60,000 Marines within 45 days into battle positions in Kuwait, all Charlie Battery knew was that every day was a training day.

Although it never made either the newspapers or the television news, the Marines had been put on notice to cross the Line of Departure (LoD) and invade Iraq on 3 March. For whatever reason, however, most likely political, the planned attack did not take place, and instead of invading Iraq that day, the Marines conducted a mobilization exercise, along with additional training missions. "We had daily rumors that we were going to invade," Phil said, "but finally, this one seemed to be true. When it turned out to be wrong, I didn't know if I was disappointed or not. We all walked around saying 'Send me to Baghdad or send me home.'"

Much of the exercises were now logistical, as the battalion finalized details on their remain-behind equipment, as well as the timetables for troop and equipment movements. Equally impor-

> Every day, it was go, then no-go. We were like, 'Take me north, or take me home!'
>
> *Cpl. Geoffrey Goodson*

tant, they checked and re-checked their lists of the equipment they expected to need on their now-imminent invasion. The following day, 4 March, was another busy day for the battery. Phil and his crew on Gun #1, along with the other Marines of 1/10, were trucked to an area outside of Camp Shoup, where they were ordered to conduct yet another exercise. On that day, they again practiced their combat skills, along with the battalion's ability to communicate and coordinate between HQ and the field batteries.

Udairi Range: more practice

These repeated training missions, known as command post (CP) exercises, and reconnaissance and selection of position drills, tested the Marines' ability to coordinate fire missions between the forward observers (FOs), the fire direction controls (FDC), the recorders, and the Marines in the CP. As an artillery battery, their ability to quickly receive and process incoming data on fire missions was of utmost importance in their ability to either return or initiate fire immediately and accurately.

Charlie, Alpha, and Bravo batteries all practiced "Red Rain" missions regularly. Red Rain is a radar-guided fire mission in which the Marine Counter-Battery Radar Detachment would spot incoming rockets and artillery fire, have their computers reverse-track the trajectories back to the launching spot, and then pass the coordinates back to FDC and the recorders back on the gun line. They also practiced moving into their next location on the LoD— a Tactical Assembly Area (TAA) called TAA Hawkins—as well as driving in their breaching lanes. They also practiced driving in the different formations they would utilize during their impending attack.

Sandstorm at Camp Shoup

Then, it was back to boredom. Had it been possible to ignore the flies, scorpions, and dung beetles, it was impossible to ignore the sandstorms. When the storms hit the camp almost daily, the world seemed to stop for Charlie Battery. Choking, swirling dust cut their vision down to a few yards, and tents often collapsed in the gale-force winds. After the storms subsided, they left a layer of dust and sand, usually on top of the dirt and sand left earlier in the day. Corporal Gallagher remembered they had to clean their gear repeatedly and field-strip and clean their M16s a couple of times a day.

Lance Corporal Turcotte hated the constant storms. "Initially, it was scary. Guys got lost inside the camp, and we joked about sending the new guys like Lubin out for food for us." But it seems the joke was on everyone because even with a line to hold on to, the flies and sand took the enthusiasm out of chow time.

Mail Call ... Finally!

It was depressing knowing that mail was such a low priority.

LCpl. Joseph Turcotte

On top of the weary waiting, blowing sandstorms, and miserable living conditions, no one had heard from their families and friends yet; the Charlie Battery Marines did not receive their first mail until 7 March—some seven weeks after leaving Camp Lejeune. Phil remembered it too well. "It really sucked. I knew my parents and friends would write, but it took almost two months from deployment until I got anything. Finally, I got a bunch from my dad, a few from my mom, and some from other relatives." Phil had plenty of lonely company.

Letter from Phil:

7 March 2003

What's up, Dad?

I finally got some mail. I got four letters from you, one from Mom, one from Grandmother & Granddad, and one from the Tavern. I can't believe all the snow you guys got. That's nuts. I'm bored. We went to the field twice to train, and other than that, we sit around. This is a weird desert.

*It's always cold, and if there are no sandstorms, it's rain-
ing. The camp we're at is like the worst one out here. The
Army has KFCs and stuff, and we eat camel for dinner.
We're supposed to invade mid to late March, but we were
also supposed to go on the 3rd, so who knows what's going
on? I just want to hurry up and do it so we can get back.
There is really nothing going on. We sleep a lot and clean
rifles because of the sandstorms and that's about it. Nice to
see where your tax dollars go. I'll talk to you later.*

No Communication Takes Its Toll

Camp Shoup did not get its own post office until about 13 March,
some three weeks after the Marines arrived. The wretched mail
service affected everyone's attitude: parents, Marines, spouses, and
girlfriends. Corporal Czombos knew his father would write because
they are quite close. Not getting any letters from him was depressing. While he kept busy, it didn't keep him from missing his dad
and brother. Laura Doggett, LCpl. Bechu's girlfriend, added, "I
got letters from Sobola that he'd written and dated Feb 24, but
were not APO postmarked until March 4. It takes 10 days to go
from one part of Kuwait to another?"

No one at home knew about these problems, so most of us
parents just kept writing and sending packages. The letters from
Col. Starnes had told us to send chapsticks, baby wipes, and other
similar products, so I made sure to include them in my care packages to Phil. I also made sure I included more disposable cameras,
cigars, matches, and more batteries for his CD player in each
package. Baby wipes for my 20-year-old Marine? I sent them. I
didn't know what he wanted, or how often he'd even receive my
packages, so I sent several small ones, instead of one or two large
packages.

From Lt. Col. Starnes' newsletters, I could see that life in
Camp Shoup was basic, which meant that it was probably rougher
than his newsletters indicated. While I was unaware that my letters
were being delayed, I was painfully cognizant that letters from Phil
were taking almost five weeks to arrive. The news broadcasts continually showed the strains and political tension between the
United States, the United Nations, Iraq, and the rest of the world.
In an attempt to keep up on the latest news bulletin, I was flicking
between MSNBC and CNN when I had TV access, and from
Yahoo to MSN when I was at work.

Although the fathers probably agonized over the details of Marine vs. Iraqi readiness, the mothers, in their own way, were equally tense. As Jamie McMillan, Phil's mother, remembered her anxiety, she began to get stressed all over again "I had terrible mood swings," she said. "As a parent, I was very proud of Phil, but I was scared to death for him as his mother. And I would have the same feelings at the same time, so I was just a wreck! It was just terrible, and living alone probably made it worse. I lived in front of the TV, and I only turned it off when I left the house."

Sharon Goodson had it a bit easier. As the wife of a former Marine, she had lived in the Marine culture for many years. "I had a lot of faith in Geoff and his training," Sharon said. "My husband is a former Marine, so I knew how well trained Geoff was. And I prayed all the time that God would keep him safe, and our friends and family prayed also. But not hearing from him was difficult; there were not many letters at all." For Lisa Santivasci, however, it was the worst of both worlds. As the wife of a career Marine, a senior NCO, she had to keep a cheerful and bright face forward for her boys, maintain a similar bright and cheerful face in the letters to her husband, and at the same time deal with all her fears and concerns privately.

In the Army camps, the troops had access to pay phones and email, and could communicate with family and friends without interruption. In a battle camp, however, those amenities were few, and our Marines were stuck with using old-fashioned mail. Everyone found the lack of family contact depressing, as Cpl. Hebert explained, "I tried hard to write to Leah, my girlfriend, every day, but once I found out that it took three days for my letters just to get to as far as Kuwait Naval Base, I knew our mail service would be shitty."

Letter from Phil:

> *11 March 2003*
>
> *Hi, Dad, what's up?*
>
> *I just found out that there's been trouble with the mail going out, so the past 3 weeks of my mail you'll probably get all at once. Mail coming in is getting better and I got a bunch from you and a couple from mom. Could you send me a 16 oz Mt. Dew and some porn and skate mags? We're not allowed to train in the field any more because the guns keep breaking and they want to save them for combat. Don't worry, I'm getting pictures! The weather is starting*

> I kept our letters to Michael light, breezy, and chatty …. I couldn't afford to have him in the middle of some battle and not be paying attention because of something I said.
>
> *Lisa Santivasci, wife*

to warm up, but we still have frequent sandstorms. Oh yeah, when we go to Iraq, there will be reporters on the gun line so there's a chance I could be on TV or in a paper. Once a week, we get a PX call, and I've saved some soda cans that have Pepsi & Coke on one side, and then Arab writing on the other. I'll bring them home with me. There's not much else going on so I'll write you again in a day or two.

Mail calls were difficult for LCpl. Warren whose mother was not much of a letter writer. "I never got used to seeing the other guys get letters when I didn't." Fortunately, parents of a friend of his, Cpl. Keane, adopted him, so he did receive some letters from them when the mail finally made its way to Camp Shoup.

While the lack of mail and packages was difficult for the Marines, it was worse for the families back home. Richard Turcotte, father of LCpl. Joseph Turcotte, had been an engineer in the regular Army and later, part of the National Guard in an artillery unit like his son. "I knew enough of what was going to happen that I stayed constantly upset. We had no mail or contact until he called us right prior to the invasion."

Leah Starner, Cpl. Hebert's fiance, had it both easier and harder than most of the other girlfriends. A girlfriend has no official standing with the Marine Corps for information, so when Lt. Col. Glenn Starnes, commanding officer of 1/10, sent his monthly newsletter, it went to Hebert's parents, who then called her with the news. But on a fortunate note for her, Hebert was one of the few Charlie Battery Marines who shipped over on USS *Portland*, whose captain gave the troops email access until they reached Kuwait. "I heard from Cory almost every day," she said, "It gave me an extra month of contact that I didn't expect." But after Hebert arrived in Kuwait, the contact stopped; it was as if he'd dropped off the face of the earth. "I wrote Cory every day," she added, "and hoped that he got them. But I didn't get any letters back until April 13, which was terrible."

Jamie Lambert related how her husband, GySgt. Lambert, and his men had been gone for over two months, but the family had not received many letters. "The Marine Corps didn't tell us anything more than the civilians knew, so Gunny's absence was especially hard on me." Two-year-old Gunner would ask constantly about his father, and usually, she had nothing to tell him. What

The mail service—it was just horrible! I checked the mail every day, hoping and praying there would be a letter from Hank.

Becky Sanders, wife

was difficult was that every time he saw a man in uniform, he'd want to know what was happening with "his daddy." Christy Fontenoy had the same type of problems with their son, Cody. "I really had nothing to tell him," she said. "Since we'd only received a few letters from John. I talked regularly with my best friend, Tammy Twiggs (a Key Volunteer and wife of SSgt. John Twiggs). She had nothing but the same PX rumors and gossip and she'd not gotten much mail from her husband, either."

For those who received mail, it was a good day. For all the others, it was another day to shrug off the hurt, and hope for a better next day. Doc Sanders said, "Getting a letter from Becky and the girls let me know they were still thinking about me. Otherwise, it's like you're out there by yourself." Corporal Czombos summed up one common sentiment among the Charlie Marines when he said, "We all looked forward to mail call."

More Waiting for War

While the Marine Corps tried to get a better handle on the problem of mail delivery, Charlie Battery trained for war. After General Conway's visit, their training increased in both pace and intensity.

For a member of a Marine artillery battery, there is more than just knowing how to fire a howitzer. There are different shells for different targets, with fuses that are set to explode at certain times. The rounds themselves are powered by charges, which are set by various strengths for various distances, and each Marine had this knowledge drummed into him at the Marine Artillery School at Fort Sill, Oklahoma.

And the Marines were still drumming this training into them at Camp Shoup. The Charlie Battery Marines reviewed and constantly trained using a variety of rounds, fuses and charges that would be used in the upcoming days.

According to Cpl. Delarosa, an artillery battery uses five types of rounds. "Each of these have a separate specific use, unless of course you run short, like we did, and then you learn to improvise!"

Dual purpose improved conventional munitions
    (DPICMs)—which are the main round the battery
    uses and feature 88 small bomblets in the nose;
High explosive (HE) rounds;
Illumination rounds—which are for night fighting;

Rocket-assisted projectile (RAP) rounds—which are for firing long distances; and

White phosphorous rounds.

Screwing on a fuse

Phil supplied the details on the four types of fuses they use to detonate a round. First, he mentioned an impact fuse, which explodes when it hits the ground. They would usually use an impact fuse with an HE round. There are two timed fuses as well: 1) a variable timed (VT) fuse, which explodes a pre-set distance from the ground and is most often used with DPICMs; and 2) a timed fuse, which detonates a fixed time after leaving the tube. Lastly, there is the concrete piercing fuse, which penetrates through four inches of solid concrete.

Corporal Hebert, the ammo team chief, explained to me about the different types of charges for which he is responsible. "The different charges relate to the distance we're required to shoot. Our smallest, or lightest charge, is a Charge 5 Green Bag. Then you graduate to a Charge 7 White, and then a Red Bag. The real monster is our Super 8 Stick, which lets us reach out and touch you at 30,000 yards (18+ miles)." Corporal Czombos added that when firing a Super 8 (the RAP round), they had to be even more prepared than normal because the concussion is so bad that after firing eight or nine rounds, "it makes you vomit; your guts actually hurt. And the recoil is enormous! When we fire with the barrel elevated, the breach almost hits the ground—it recoils almost five feet!"

Consequently, the gun crews trained hard. Lance Corporal Turcotte talked about how GySgt. "Gunny" Lambert came up with ideas on laying their guns that cut their set-up time in half. "Maybe it was because he had experience in Desert Storm, or probably that's why he's the Gunny, but it worked, and we cut our time in half." In actuality, they cut their time from the normal twelve minutes down to an incredible four minutes! This was an eight-minute advantage that would be put to good use in the coming days.

Gunny Lambert had trained on 105s howitzers and other weapons systems in his younger days, plus he'd had Marines who had fought in Vietnam teach

Artillery rounds and fuses on pallets

him the ropes. These experiences, in addition to those he'd picked up in Desert Storm, helped him learn "a few tricks" for his Marines. He knew the training was repetitive and boring, but he never stopped drilling the battery, explaining, "They didn't yet understand how our constant training is the difference between the Marines and everyone else …. When the fighting starts, and you're all nervous and scared, that's when your training takes over, and you get the job done." Like Gunny, 1st Lt. Shea had seen action in Desert Storm and understood what was needed for their training. "When you're exhausted or scared, or both, that's the time your training kicks in, and that's when you win your battle, and stay alive."

Marine units—whether infantry, artillery, amphibious assault vehicles, or armor—work best on the move. So the three batteries practiced a concept known as "Hip Shots" where they were driving through the desert in their 7-ton trucks, towing their gun, and they'd practice a sudden stop, and they'd leap out, set up the gun—quick! quick!—and be ready to fire.

The training emphasis was different at Camp Shoup. At home, or on the float, they trained hard, but safety was emphasized more. "Not that we did anything dangerous," explained LCpl. Turcotte, "but the emphasis now was on speed, instead of safety. If we could set up and lay the guns faster, and begin counter-fire faster, that's what we needed to do, and that's what we practiced."

Everyone trained. When they weren't in the field, Doc Sanders and the other corpsmen were in the battalion aid station (BAS), where they would run triage exercises. For example, they would be told five Marines were down, and then they'd have to decide who to save first, what to do, and who to evacuate. Sanders added, "Four or more dead Marines were considered a mass casualty, to be handled a certain way. Any chemical attack deaths were considered to be 'dirty bodies,' and they would be handled a special way. This was serious training. The guys in the field were my friends, so I stayed focused on what they were teaching us. I'd be ready if they needed me."

> By the time Gunny was finished with us, we could get a round off, accurately of course, in five minutes. We knew our stuff cold!
>
> *Cpl. Chris Gault*

> In training, safety is better. In war, speed is better, and Gunny taught us well.
>
> *LCpl. Joseph Turcotte*

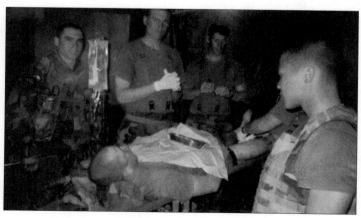

Doc and the first aid team performing a mock operation

As studying and training intensified at the BAS, an order from Battalion HQ got Sanders' attention. The order demanded each man be issued small bags so he could collect and carry a dead Marine's personal effects. If the bags didn't arrive in time, then they were to give out zip-lock baggies. Corporal Goodson also noticed how the situation seemed to suddenly get more serious. "We were told we should carry any personal items in our cargo pocket, so if we were killed, whoever found us could cut it open and bring our stuff home. That opened my eyes."

Breaks in the Monotony

While Charlie Battery trained regularly, and cleaned their guns even more regularly, they maintained an upbeat attitude. Not surprisingly, and probably in view of their ages, they made their own fun with a typical Marine sense of humor. Many of the Marines thought the desert animals were great entertainment. One such "entertaining" example was the practice of catching scorpions and placing them in a ring, where they would fight one another. When the fight was over, they would save the winner for the next bout. The scarabs did their fair share in entertaining the troops too. Some Marines would catch the big beetles and make them race each other. The loser paid a heavy price: death by fire. Desert lizards roamed the camp and could cause a diversion one way or another. Phil told a story of how Section Chief Wilson caught one of the lizards by hitting it with a mallet, and others threw it in the fire. "No one would eat it though, no matter how much we offered to pay them!"

More maturely, and as a morale builder, Chaps Ritchie, who had brought his bagpipes along with him, played regularly for everyone to enjoy. He played "Scotland the Brave," "The Black Bear," and all the other traditional Scottish melodies. But regardless of what he played, he always finished with "Amazing Grace."

In between "playing" with the desert wildlife and listening to music, every now and then an exciting episode would stir up certain parts of the camp. For example, one afternoon there was

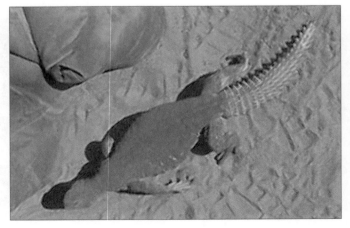

One of the many lizards that made its home in camp

some brief excitement when Cpl. Delarosa somehow managed to inject himself with an NBC antidote. This brought the corpsmen and the other Marines running to the scene, both to watch and to break the monotony. "I'm still not sure how it went off," Delarosa explained, "but the needle went thru all three layers of clothing and my MOPP suit. I caught a lot of shit from my friends, of course, so I told them that I was just trying to see if all the NBC stuff really worked."

Otherwise, life in Camp Shoup bordered on tedious. The Marines played cards constantly; often, they played wearing their gas masks. They wrote letters home that they assumed would eventually be delivered, and waited to be told what was the next drill or the next training exercise.

Gas Masks, MOPPs & Staying Fit

Charlie Battery continued their training missions, as they trucked into the desert for another live-fire exercise, and continued their virtually daily gas attack practice. Lance Corporal Lamb remembered how "Someone would call 'gas-gas-gas,' and we'd rip our masks out, and get them on. We slept with our masks within arm's reach; they drummed NBC preparation into us constantly."

> Our masks didn't stop everything we learned about. They'd stop nerve agents, but none of the funky stuff.
>
> *Cpl. Justin Noyes*

They were required to keep their masks within arm's reach; they were told that in case of a gas attack, they had nine seconds to don them; a nine-second margin between life and death. Not surprisingly, wearing gas masks became a normally accepted part of their routine. Eventually, both to acclimate the Marines to their gear, and to keep them safe from an Iraqi pre-emptive WMD strike, Charlie Battery and the other Marines at Camp Shoup wore their MOPPs and gas masks constantly. With the exception of eating, the Marines kept their masks on throughout the day. Phil looked at wearing his mask as part of this unique Camp Shoup environment. "It took some time to get used to wearing them when we just walking around, but I guess since everyone wore them, it didn't matter that we all looked like we were in a science fiction film."

Bechu wearing his gas mask

The month of training in the desert had done its job in making these fit Marines even fitter. The amount of gear each Marine carried was staggering: M16, helmet, ammunition, two canteens, Kevlar flak jacket on the outside, and in their packs, they carried their clothing, personal items, trenching shovel, and sleeping bags. I remembered my amazement at the weight of Phil's gear the night I put it on back in the barracks; to hike with all this—and be able to fight—in the loose desert terrain; these Marines had to be both fit and motivated.

Waiting for Word on the Home Front

While our Charlie Battery Marines were fit and motivated, the parents back home agonized over the daily and hourly cable news. I downloaded and printed every Marine-related Yahoo. AltaVista, and MSNBC article I could find, and I then called everyone I knew and read them the articles. Paul Czombos, father of Michael, felt as helpless as I did and also felt he was not being productive at his job. "I couldn't concentrate on anything other than the upcoming war. I lived from broadcast to broadcast on MSNBC, CNN, and Fox, either at home or at work."

No news is not really good news when your son goes off to war. While the Marine Corps recognized that too much news could cause a security breach, too little news caused unnecessary stress on the home front. Stressed and anxious letters from home could easily affect the performance of the Marines in the field, which could cause Marine casualties. Therefore, Col. Starnes' HQ back in Camp Lejeune sent every spouse and parent a Contact Phone List, which was a list of phone numbers and people to contact for information. They also included a 2nd MEB Hotline, as well as a website. The hotline phone number was usually busy when I called it, which meant that I wasn't the only anxious parent out there.

So while our Marines were training hard and staying busy, the stress on the parents and wives back at home increased as the days and news escalated. Perhaps surprisingly, the Charlie Battery wives back at Camp Lejeune received no more information than we parents had. No one, either on-base or off, received any confidential or otherwise "hot" information. It makes perfect sense in retrospect, but I found it hard to believe at the time. However, the Marine Corps had studied and interviewed many Marines and their spouses after Desert Storm, and they came up with a tremendous support system for the wives and children of the deployed troops, as well as for the parents.

I was consumed with the news. At home, it was just me and my TV.

Paul Czombos, father

This system of support consisted of Key Volunteers (KVs). The KV concept gave all spouses or parents—regardless of whether they lived on-base or not—an "official" contact with the Marine Corps. These contacts were distributed by battery, regiment, and division. For Charlie Battery wives, GySgt. Lambert's wife, Jamie, was a KV; whereas, MSgt. Santivasci's wife, Lisa, worked with the younger wives in HQ. Mrs. Ferah Shea, 1st Lt. Shea's wife, was the Charlie Battery Coordinator, and therefore, talked to the parents of the Charlie Battery Marines.

Mrs. Jamie Lambert was proud to talk about her role in the KV program. She described herself as "a mother hen" for her group of young wives who were mostly 18 and 19 years old, and while she often had little or no news to share with them, she felt she had to be strong for them to reduce their stress and worry. It was a challenge to be convincing since she had no idea what their husbands were doing and what was happening to them, but she said, "I had to convince them that my husband and the Marine Corps would keep their husbands safe."

As a KV volunteer, Mrs. Lisa Santivasci recalled her duties initially were "some basic hand-holding, and cheering up a few worried wives." But just before the war started, the KVs held a meeting and they were told to get a phone number and exact physical address for every moment of the day for every one of their wives. They wanted this precise information in the event one of their husbands got killed, the Marine Corps could reach the wives and families with the Notification Team before any media did. At that meeting, "It truly dawned on me how real this was."

Reality of the eventual invasion was hitting everyone hard by this time. Phil's 20th birthday was 15 March 2003. The TV news, coupled with the lack of letters from him, made it an extremely unpleasant day for me. I'd sent him two packages several weeks prior, along with several birthday cards, in the hopes that he'd get at least one of them on time. It would have been nice to hear directly from him how he was faring, instead of trying to extrapolate his doings off of sporadic Yahoo or MSN Internet articles. On that night, drinking one bottle of wine led to a second bottle, as I sat at my desk and wrote him yet another letter. I remembered when Phil was born, and the evening my father and I sat down and demolished a fair quantity of wine, and brandy, in his honor as the first son and grandson. It had been an excellent dinner 20 years ago, and I could only sit there that night with MSNBC on the TV, and some Irish music in the background, and hope that my father was looking in on him, and would bring him home safe, and with distinction.

What I didn't know, as I sat and worried at my desk that night, was that Phil and the battery had been sent back to the Udairi Training Range on 15 March for their final exercise. By this time, Charlie Battery had honed their fighting and survival skills to a sharp edge, and this exercise was more fine-tuning than out-and-out training. From siting their guns quickly and accurately, to desert convoy movements, to battery-battalion communications, 1st Lt. Shea, Top Santivasci, Gunny Lambert, and SSgt. Fontenoy had Phil and the others as primed and trained for whatever battle-field situation they could imagine.

The Marines of Charlie Battery had traveled a long way, both physically and emotionally since their 1 January recall to Camp Lejeune. While they still had no idea when or how the war would start, they did know they were ready to go. Steeped in the tradition of the Marine Corps, they were prepared to fight, and were beginning to be increasingly frustrated at their continued training in the desert. As cut off from civilization as they were, with no news, and mail just beginning to straggle in, they had no idea of what was happening "back in the world" and how that was about to change their future.

Chapter 5

Invasion Force

Does my country really understand that this is World War III ...?
We have to fight hard and land safely. We have to fight the
terrorists as if there were no rules, and preserve our
open society as if there were no terrorists. It won't
be easy. It will require our best strategies, our
most creative diplomats, and our
bravest soldiers. Semper Fi.

Thomas Friedman*

**Kuwaiti Desert
17–21 March 2003**

On Monday evening, 17 March 2003, President George W. Bush
addressed the American public and the world. In his brief, 15-
minute speech, he told Saddam Hussein and his sons they had 48
hours to leave Iraq and go into exile, or face an overwhelming and
immediate attack. Arms inspectors, diplomats, journalists, and
other civilians were warned to leave the country immediately.
There was no immediate response from the Iraqi leader, and in
any event, Mr. Bush's language and tone suggested he did not
expect him to comply. President Bush did not announce a date for
the commencement of the war, but he made it clear that he would
act as soon as his deadline expired on Wednesday, 19 March, or
sooner, if he felt it necessary.

The waiting for war was over, and the diplomatic wrangling
and vote trading in the United Nations' Security Council finally
ceased—Chile bartering its vote for NAFTA membership; Mexico
horsetrading its vote for an immigration deal; Russia abstaining

---

* *The New York Times*, September 13, 2001.

from the vote or not; and France criticizing America and Great Britain yet again. Abruptly, all the political posturing and procrastination had come to a halt, and the Marines would solve the Saddam problem their own definitive way.

When the president finally said, "Let's go!" and the world watched the cruise missiles and B-52s roaring towards Baghdad, I wouldn't be concentrating on this made-for-television war. Instead, I would be thinking of Phil and his buddies in Charlie Battery grinding through the Iraqi desert in their 7-ton trucks. The real war wouldn't be CNN-friendly and TV-sterile; I was sure the real war would be decided by Phil, Hebert, Bechu, Turcotte, Warren, Souza, and the others on Gun #1; Barr and Gallagher on Gun #2; Jones and Gault on Gun #3; Cpl. Czombos and Cpl. Delarosa on Gun #5, and Noyes on Gun #6. This is where the casualties are taken, not in the B-52s.

These Marines, most of them between ages 20–24, would be on the gun line, as were many of their fathers and grandfathers before them. There was absolutely no doubt in my mind they'd acquit themselves well against any Iraqi troops, be they Republican Guard, regular army, or Fedayeen.

This was all fine, but the sick feeling in my stomach came from thinking about the potential cost. America and the world now passed beyond the boundaries of a "possible" war, and if the Bush administration was remotely correct in its WMD scenario, Phil and his friends on Gun #1, and the rest of the Marines in Charlie Battery and throughout Task Force Tarawa, would suffer terribly in a WMD attack.

It's a Go!

Charlie Battery had been on another field op, a live-fire practice upcountry at the Udairi Training Range. They had been out for two days when the president spoke, so the Marine Command recalled them to Camp Shoup. Gunnery Sergeant Lambert confidently recalled how "We were told to be ready to go on a 24-hour notice, but I had them ready to go on about two hours' notice."

The tone in Camp Shoup was electric as the anticipation of finally getting to do what they were sent to do coursed through the camp. Keeping that electricity charged was the news Charlie Battery Marines were hearing on 1st Lt. Shea's radio, which he had brought with him to Kuwait. First Lieutenant Shea, a veteran

Monday, 17 March 2003
D Minus 4

of Desert Storm, knew what to expect in the coming days, and he knew it was important to have the men know what was happening. Corporal Goodson, for one, was grateful for the BBC news reports he and the others heard. "It kept us in the loop, and I found that knowing what was going on around me was a real morale booster."

By 1000 that morning, copies of the president's speech were being passed through the troops at Camp Shoup. Not many of the Marines had stayed awake to listen to the speech, which was delivered at 0500 local time, but the speech was the major topic of conversation a few hours later. At last, they would either fight or go home—and the destination would be decided for them quickly.

Most everyone agreed that having the waiting and the ceaseless training over was a relief. They were going to finally be able to put all their skill and hard work to the test. No more beetle races, lizard lashings, or scorpion fights. They were now going to be fighting and they were ready. Corporal Czombos summed it up for his friends and fellow Marines, "The waiting around camp was the hardest part. There is a big difference between being ready and staying ready. Man, we were ready!"

> **I joined the Marines to fight, and I was ready to fight.**
>
> *LCpl. Sobola Bechu*

With more than 250,000 American and British troops stationed in Kuwait, Bahrain, and Qatar—and four Naval Task Forces in the Persian Gulf, Arabian Gulf, and the Red Sea—President Bush controlled a force that was measurably more powerful than those his father commanded in Desert Storm. There was no doubt as to the efficiency of the Allied force; the big question was how well would the Iraqis fight back, and would they use their infamous and enormous inventory of WMD?

As Paul Czombos, Becky Sanders, Lisa Santivasci, Christy and Cody Fontenoy, and all of the other parents and wives watched the news channels back in America, the many television armchair generals debated cloud levels over Iraq, ambient desert humidity levels, and other extraneous variables to prove their military knowledge and increase their audience share. While it was important only to them as to who beat who in the ratings, their greatest success lay in scaring the parents and wives of the American troops involved with their supposed WMD and Republican Guard troop expertise.

Many of the Marine wives found these scare tactics both unnecessary and unwelcome. as Mrs. Lisa Santivasci related, "Although I was a TV addict when Michael fought in Desert

Storm, this time, with the boys, I could not watch the television so constantly again. There were too many opinions and commentaries on TV that were frightening." So she made a deal with her two sons, Michael and Raymond. She agreed to watch TV twice a day, and she would give them a brief report as to what she heard. She felt the boys didn't need to be seeing and hearing all that was being revealed on the television. After speaking to the boys' teachers, they agreed to help keep the war news to a minimum as well. Since the boys both attended a school on base, many of their friends had a father who was deployed to fight too. The teachers did an excellent job of understanding their parents' concerns. The school principal did a good job of keeping the focus on their academics because much of the war news was simply unhealthy for elementary and junior high students.

But back in Kuwait, in the cold and windy confines of Camp Shoup, our Marines knew nothing of the ratings games back home. For them, this was no game, and they packed their personal gear, checked and cleaned their 155mms and M16s yet again, and were told to write to their families and loved ones. For Charlie Battery, the four-week wait in the desert was over. In Camp Shoup, our Marines packed their gear one more time, but this time, they were ordered to pack the personal items they planned to leave behind, and then stored them in alphabetical order in a giant shipping container.

Charlie Battery readying their vehicles

"The Death Letter"

After stowing their personal gear, they had one more assignment to complete, which finally served to convince them that they were finally going off to fight. Known in the Marine Corps as "The Letter," or more accurately, "The Death Letter," each Marine was instructed to write a "To Whom it May Concern" letter to his parents, wife, or other loved one. Writing this letter was not required, but the Marine Corps strongly recommended it, and the Charlie Battery Marines listened and obeyed; albeit, with varying attitudes.

Gunnery Sergeant Lambert and SSgt. Fontenoy went to each member of Charlie Battery and made sure each of them had a letter written, which was then put away for safekeeping.

Writing the letter drew mixed opinions from Phil and his friends. Personally, Phil didn't want to write a letter because he thought it was bad luck. On the other hand, Cpl. Hebert wrote his letter with a different frame of mind: if he had to write such a letter, he wanted it to be a "good one." When asked what he wrote, he deferred the question saying that it didn't matter what he'd written, because he'd come home. For some, the toughest part of writing the letter was finding the right words. Corporal Czombos wrote a letter to his father, but it felt awkward. "What do you say? It's official. I'm dead. I love you."

Corporal Turcotte ended up writing two death letters, one he gave to the Marine Corps, the other he mailed to his father, Richard, who remembered receiving the letter and admitted, "It was the first letter we'd received from him since he deployed in January, and I just could not open it. I knew what it was, and what it represented."

Chaplain Ritchie knew what writing the letter represented. A veteran of Desert Storm and Afghanistan, he knew what was coming, and therefore, he and his fellow chaplains made themselves even more available for the Marines and were busier than ever. All the chaplains took a very active role during this time and they met with as many Marines as wanted to see them. "There were a lot of calls for us, both loud and soft, as we walked through the lines. There were a lot of Marines with big eyes during those days." As the war loomed and the death letters were being written, young Marines called out to any chaplain who passed by. It didn't matter to them who was from what faith. Just because Ritchie was an Anglican Methodist, that didn't stop his Catholic Marines from asking him to bless their medals. He said, "Of course I did; I blessed a lot of medals those days."

After all the weeks of training in the desert, some of Charlie Battery looked at "The Letter" as a sort of an initial call-to-action. Corporal Goodson said, "When they told us to go write

I heard a lot of 'Hey Chaps, got a minute for me?'

Chaplain Gordon Ritchie

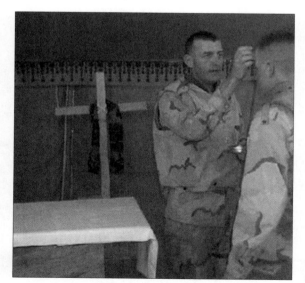

Chaps Ritchie performing Ash Wednesday service

one, then it began to dawn on me that we were going to move out; that our training was really done. Only now did I believe we were going to fight."

Private Barr's letter-writing took him back to Belleau Wood in France where he had visited a spring that had refreshed those famous WWI Marines, including Dan Daily. Legend had it, if a person drank from its waters, he would live forever. As he wrote his letter, he remembered drinking from this spring and hoped very much that the legend was true.

The "Devildog" spring at Belleau Wood

Families Prepare Themselves for War

As our Charlie Battery Marines wrote the letters they hoped would not be mailed, we parents, wives, and girlfriends also realized the time for diplomacy and negotiation had come to an end. Mrs. Lisa Santivasci's father was a flight surgeon on USS *Oriskany*, an aircraft carrier stationed off the Vietnamese coast. She related how he would never talk about what he saw as a war doctor, and that made her worry even more about her husband, Michael, and what could happen to him. "The uncertainty of the whole mess was just eating me alive."

Like Mrs. Santivasci, Paul Czombos remembers the stress of this time period too. His son, Mike, was able to call him when they were striking camp and getting ready to leave for the line of departure. Mike described to him the battery was loading its gear and that their training had them ready to fight. "I told him to be careful, and that I loved him. And he said the same to me."

For my own part, I assumed that Bush would start with an air war, and after a few days of the promised "shock and awe air campaign," he'd unleash the troops. My initial reaction was not too dissimilar than Phil's and rest of Charlie Battery's. "Don't give Saddam any 48-hour notice!" I yelled at the television screen that night. "Just fucking go!"

At this point, the Rules of Engagement (ROE) experienced a major change. While on shipboard, the ROE classes talked about warnings, moderation, and the Geneva Convention, but with the invasion close at hand, the Marines were told the emphasis was safety—theirs. "Use your judgment," SSgt. Fontenoy told them, "but if he has a weapon, it's a choice between you and him, so

I was relieved and excited about getting to fight, but I was still nervous about doing my job.

LCpl. Sobola Bechu

make sure you kill him. You should assume that every Iraqi male is an enemy, and use your head accordingly."

This Is No Drill!

Camp Shoup was suddenly even busier than those first days when the Marines arrived and built the camp. As the Marines struck their tents and looked to their gear one more time, the staff sergeants eye-balled their guns and equipment. Charlie Battery packed and recounted all their spares; once again, they counted and packed their tires, welding sets, chains, shovels, medical supplies, ammunition, and rations. They'd been performing the same routine since the first week of January when they packed their gear back at Camp Lejeune, but for the first time, they knew it was no drill.

Letter from Phil:

18 March 2003

What's up, Dad?

I got your tattoo magazine today. Thanks! It's nice to have magazines to look at since the sand broke my CD player. We were in the field for the past three days and they called us in early because we're on standby to go. Bush gave Saddam 48 hours to leave, so if he stays, we go in, blow things up, and if he leaves, we go in and act as peacekeepers. So either way, I should be in Iraq in the next couple of days. It's about time. I want to kill some Iraqis. They gave us a 12-hour window to be ready when we're called, but all we need is about 45 minutes. Oh yeah, since we left, we shot our rifles once on the boat, but here, we shot the .50 cals and the M203 grenade launchers. That was cool. Not much else. So hopefully, my next letter will be written in Iraq.

To make the the final hours pass, the Marines played cards, wrote letters, and as nerves would allow, tried to sleep.

Phone Home!

On 19 March, Charlie Battery and all the other units of 1/10 received their orders. They were to break camp and get ready to move the next day from Camp Shoup to TAA Hawkins (their assault point). The Marines repacked their seabags for the umpteenth time, and made sure they were properly identified, and then stashed them in the big 40-foot shipping containers that were being used for storage.

The welcome appearance of telecommunications technology on the scene became a wonderfully timely tool, as suddenly, many Marines had an unexpected opportunity to call home. Their 2nd Marine Expeditionary Brigade (MEB) Command had bought six mobile phones and preprogrammed them for three-minute calls home. Needless to say, these "Morale Phones" were an instant hit with the troops. As the RCT-2 Battalion chaplain, Chaps Ritchie signed for the phones and had the enjoyable chore of bringing them to the Marines. "You can be a rough and tough Marine, and still want to call and talk to your wife or girlfriend before you go and fight."

> I talked to both my mom and dad; I had no idea when I might be able to talk to them again.
>
> *LCpl. Joseph Turcotte*

For a few parents back home, the morale phones were a lifeline back to their sons. Paul Czombos received a surprise call from his son, who told him how they were loading their gear in order to move up to the LoD. "This was a special call," he said. "While Mike's letters were a godsend, to actually hear him just made me proud of him to the point of tears." Lucille Warren was at work when she received a call from her son, Carl. She was thrilled that he had called her, but the line was so bad she could barely hear him. Unfortunately, what should have been a happy experience only made her frustrated and very angry. "I couldn't hear what he was trying to tell me!"

With only six telephones for the troops, many of the Marines did not get the chance to call home, especially if they were already engaged in a work party. Many were also packing their personal gear. They had to decide on what personal gear to take and what to leave behind. Most wanted to bring their cameras, CDs, and batteries. Since packs could be stashed in the trucks, they didn't have to worry about the weight as much. Any items that were left behind had to be properly tagged, so when they returned from Iraq—whenever that was expected to be—they could pick up their belongings.

In addition, all the military equipment not being used for the next day's invasion was cleaned, packed, and staged for future use, and then vehicles and equipment that would be used was staged and readied for the drive to TAA Hawkins.

Not knowing whether their Iraqi opponents would either stand and fight, or run, the Marine Corps used every motivational tool at its disposal to make sure each Marine had the right attitude for the upcoming war. This included reminders of 2nd Marine Division's history and tradition. The names Hawkins and Shoup were no accidents. The Tactical Assault Area (TAA) was named for 1st Lt. William Dean Hawkins, a 2nd Marine Division Marine who won the Medal of Honor posthumously at Tarawa in November 1943. The camp was named after another 2nd Marine Division Medal of Honor winner at Tarawa, Col. David M. Shoup, later General David Shoup, the 22nd Commandant of the Marine Corps.

The Convoy to TAA Hawkins

Thursday, 20 March 2003
D minus 1

The weather conditions deteriorated quickly that morning. The winds kicked up yet again, and visibility dropped appreciably as the desert windstorms drove dust and sand into the Marines' eyes and ears, and under their already-dirty clothing. Charlie Battery spent the morning sitting in their Humvees or their 7-tons, as they awaited the order to move out. Finally, at 1035, 1st Lt. Shea was given the word to move out, and Charlie Battery—already in their MOPP gear—checked their howitzers, looked yet again to their M16s, and began the 4 1/2-hour drive north to their staging point, a few klicks (kilometers) south of the Kuwaiti-Iraqi border.

As they moved up to their staging point at TAA Hawkins, a quiet atmosphere prevailed in the trucks. Lieutenant Shea remarked, "They were getting their game faces on; they were all very serious." When I asked Phil and his buddy, Cpl. Justin Noyes, about the ride to Hawkins, a sudden and somber silence fell over my office. Even after several months, the memory of that ride north evoked a subdued reaction. Phil quietly recalled, "There was no trash-talking on the ride up. This trip was for real, and we all knew it." The swirling dust that shrouded the truck only added to making the long, rough ride more isolating and tense. Noyes remembers, "There

Moving out to TAA Hawkins

were some jokes, but more to break the tension, than anything really funny. It was no time to bullshit."

Traffic was extremely heavy as the thousands of vehicles involved in the invasion moved up to their respective jumping-off points on the border. In addition to the 1/10 artillery convoy, Phil, LCpl. Bechu, Cpl. Noyes, and Cpl. Czombos, and the others could look out of their 7-tons and sometimes see their fellow Marines of Task Force Tarawa moving up with them. The constant roar of the diesel engines from all the 7-ton trucks, AAVs, the tanks and the noise of the battery guns being towed consumed their dust-filled, mobile world. "It was so loud," Czombos remembered. "But with this giant convoy around me, I got more motivated the more I looked around!"

Although Phil's world and that of his friends existed primarily in the realm of his gun and from what he could see from the back of his 7-ton; in the bigger picture, there were even more Marines on the move up to the LoD. Off in the distance, and seen only as huge blowing clouds of dust and sand, were the Marines of the 1st Marine Division (from Camp Pendleton) who were also moving up to their respective destinations.

As Charlie Battery rolled to TAA Hawkins that morning, they moved in a specific order. This was the driving column called "Desert Wedge" they'd practiced back on the Udairi Training Range.

The first (or point) Humvee in the column was 1st Lt. Shea's with Cpl. Goodson at the wheel and Cpl. Aguila manning the .50 cal. in the ring mount for security. They were the lead vehicle, so if any shooting started, they'd be involved first. Following behind Lt. Shea's vehicle was the 7-ton truck pulling Gun #1, with Cpl. Souza driving, and Phil, Hebert, Bechu, Turcotte, and the others seated in the rear of the truck. Their ammo truck followed them, then another 7-ton with fire direction control (FDC) was directly behind them. Next in line was Gun #2, followed by their ammo truck. Each subsequent gun had an ammo truck behind it. The remainder of the battery—radar direction control (RDC), spares, food, HQ (with Top Santivasci and Chaps Ritchie), and all the others—followed the howitzers on their way to their staging point.

They drove across the Kuwaiti desert until early afternoon when their journey ended at TAA Hawkins. TAA Hawkins—which was not even a camp, but rather a spot on the map—was only six klicks (3.25 miles) off the LoD, and upon arrival, Charlie Battery

We were fully suited up with masks, boots, and gloves. So it was easy to stay quiet.

Cpl. Justin Noyes

and the other Marines of 1/10 and Task Force Tarawa were ordered to disembark from their 7-tons and to dig fighting pits. "We were a tired-looking group of Marines," Phil said. "We'd been driving over some pretty rough terrain, and the back of a 7-ton is not very comfortable. We'd been bounced around for the last four hours, and I was relieved to finally get out." This was especially true since the Marines had spent the previous night sleeping in their truck, which meant nobody logged enough rest. The lack of sleep, the rigors of the long ride, and the tension of the upcoming action combined to make many uptight. "But at least we knew we were finally going to fight," Cpl. Gault added.

> Adrenaline goes a long way, but we'd been on edge for a while, and some of us were a little goofy.
>
> *Cpl. Chris Gault*

The Line of Departure (LoD)

The LoD was a spot on the borderline between Iraq and Kuwait. The border was delineated by giant sand berms that had been built by the Kuwaitis after Operation Desert Storm. These dunes had been bulldozed up to a height of 15 to 20 feet, and they stretched the 124 miles of shared border between the two countries. Two of these huge sand walls, which resembled a sandy Great Wall of China, were built parallel to each other, and in between the two sand walls, was an electrified fence. Additionally, barbed wire, concertina wire, and other impediments to easy access had been added on top of each sand wall. While the berms were solid when built, huge holes had been just been bulldozed in them by the Marine engineers and the Kuwaiti contractors, so that the armored forces, trucks, and troops could pour through them when so ordered.

In the preceding days, on or about 14 March, the television news had reported that some UN observers had come across soldiers with heavy equipment bulldozing holes in the berms. Although both the television and print news claimed the soldiers identified themselves as Marines, the report disappeared quickly and quietly. The breaches in the berms remained open.

After Charlie Battery and Task Force Tarawa arrived at the LoD, they once again staged themselves in their driving order for the next day's invasion. The 2nd Light Armored Reconnaissance (LAR) Battalion was tasked to lead off, then infantry, then 1/10's artillery, and then more infantry, and HQ and the support groups. First Lieutenant Shea's Humvee led, followed by Phil and the others on Gun #1, Gun #2, and the others, Armor and LAVs were arrayed off on the flanks. Off to the west lay the 1st Marine Expeditionary Force (MEF), who was finishing their own staging operations, as they pulled into their assault points. "This was a huge fucking convoy," said Cpl. Czombos, "I was almost jumping up and down with nerves and excitement when I looked out the sides of my truck. There were just hundreds of fucking vehicles coming with us!"

Once they finished digging their fighting pits, they opened up their MREs and ate. Phil was quiet as he remembered how "I checked my M16 for probably the hundredth time that day. I didn't talk much; I really didn't know what to say. I just kind of sat and worried about what would happen next."

With President Bush's deadline set to expire, the Iraqis took him at his word and began launching Scuds sporadically throughout the night.

Iraqi & American "Fireworks"

No one in Charlie Battery really slept that night. After the Marines scraped their fighting holes out of the rough ground, they sat and picked at their food and contemplated the next day's invasion. The cold desert wind continued to blow, and many of the Marines kept their MOPP masks on for most of the night.

Thursday evening, 20 March 2003

D minus 1/2

At the LoD that night, more than 60,000 Marines—the largest and most powerful operation in Marine history—stretched along a 25-mile length of berms and barbed wire. Amongst the Task Force was my son and his friends: a group of young men mentally readying themselves to fight their first war. Even the experienced officers and senior NCOs, like 1st Lt. Shea, Top Santivasci, and Gunny Lambert, sat and wondered about the days ahead. Yet in the middle of this mass of weaponry and worry, a few individuals stepped forward to help calm the troops and set their minds right.

Chaps Ritchie was one of those Marines. Although he had played his bagpipes every night in Camp Shoup, the music now took on a special meaning on this last night before Phil and the others rolled through the berms and into Iraq. As the sun set on Charlie Battery, Chaps walked out past the Marines and their vehicles, and like one of the Scottish pipers of old, stood alone and played for his men. Lance Corporal Turcotte recalls how "he played 'Amazing Grace' for like 20 minutes. It was just incredible, that music, and that instrument. Even talking about it today gives me chills all over again."

I thought about Becky and my girls, and about all the shit the Iraqis might use, and I didn't sleep.

PO3 Doc Sanders

They must have fired 30+ Scuds over us, and with our missiles firing back, it was an exciting night!

LCpl. Nicholas Lamb

As one of the senior NCOs, SSgt. Fontenoy also needed to check on his Marines and reassure them that all was well that night. He walked the line that evening "just to see how they all were doing. Everyone was edgy, but they all assured me they were fine." Lieutenant Colonel Starnes had come by earlier as well and given Charlie Battery a short talk, confirming with the men that they were well-trained, that they were Marines and they would do well.

In the early evening, the Army launched a massive barrage of Army Tactical Missiles (ATACMs) and Multiple Rocket Launching Systems (MRLSs). This was in support of the 1st MEF Marines and various Army troops as they crossed the LoD from their assault points some 15 miles away. Staff Sergeant Fontenoy recalled telling his edgy Charlie Battery Marines, "Those missiles are our support. Our 1st MEF Marines are moving now, so get ready; we'll be rolling with them soon." The MRLSs lit up the sky for Charlie Battery and the Task Force Tarawa Marines. The Iraqis launched a few of their Scud missiles in a desultory defense of their country, and our Charlie Battery Marines sat and watched the sound and light show. More than a few Marines, already edgy with adrenaline and fatigue, mistook the outbound ATACMs for inbound Scuds, and called in gas alerts. The Marine Command, therefore, ordered the donning of MOPP gear, and the Marines spent a cold and sleepless night watching the missile exchange.

With the exchange of missiles lighting up night sky, no one really slept much. Lance Corporal Bechu concurred. "It was fucking great. These things kept coming overhead, going wherever into Kuwait, and then our Patriots replied and blew those fuckers up. I doubt anyone slept!" Then he added, "This was the time I was most scared, Sir. We were just at the mercy of some Scud dropping out of the sky on us." Many of the Charlie Battery Marines thought they'd seen dozens of Scud missiles coming in over them.

In reality, 1st Lt. Shea confirmed less than a dozen Scuds actually came overhead. When told of their reactions to that night of noise and nerves, Lt. Shea laughed and said, "Well, this was their first combat, and they were pretty nervous, even though they all tried hard not to show it. We had maybe 8–10 Scuds come overhead, very high up. You could hear them, but not see them. What they saw were our MRLSs being shot back."

During that night, Cpl. Hebert described how several of his buddies were all crouching in a big fighting hole when suddenly, one of them, LCpl. Kowalski, stood up and shouted, "Look!

Fireworks!" Hebert said, "SSgt. Twiggs went crazy and shouted, 'Get that stupid fucker down!' So someone grabbed Kowalski and hauled him down so he wouldn't get hurt."

During the night's rocket attack, Pvt. Barr recounted how he remembered what his father, a Marine veteran of Vietnam, had told him before he left back in January. "'There is a fine line between bravery and stupidity,' he'd said. Now I began to understand what he meant."

A memorable moment for Cpl. Czombos was when a cruise missile streaked overhead at a height of less than 100 feet. "This thing just roared up out of the dark, all sparks and noise, right on the deck. We all just about shit! No one had any fucking idea of what it was, until Gunny or someone told us what it was. I bet it really sucked to be on the receiving end of it!"

And So It Begins ...

As the cold morning sun rose on 21 March, Charlie Battery was again reminded to wear their bulky MOPP gear. Accordingly, they donned their gas masks, and they each carried their protective boots and gloves with them. Carrying their M16s, Phil and the others walked stiffly to their trucks, mounted up, and waited for the order to roll. The lead elements of Task Force Tarawa began to move at 1045 that morning, and the long lines of M1 Abrams tanks, amphibious assault vehicles (AAVs), and the 7-tons towing their deadly M198 155mm howitzers, began to form up and move out.

Friday, 21 March 2003

Of course, none of us at home knew any of this. I had just stayed glued to the television or the Internet and trolled for any news of the expected onset of hostilities. "It was like being paralyzed," said Nancy Turcotte, "or living in slow-motion. I knew what was about to happen, but I just couldn't bring myself to admit that my son was about to be in the middle of it." Despite her role as a Key Volunteer, Lisa Santivasci received no more details on her husband's whereabouts or activities than any of us civilians. "I was watching a taped show on the TV with my boys," she said, "when a neighbor called and told me the war started, so now we had no choice but to watch; it was on every station. I hugged the boys, and reminded them again and again, about how Daddy was such an awesome Marine."

War protests continued to erupt around the world, and around the United States. Weekend protest rallies were announced for

Our lifeline was knowing how well trained he was. We all reminded each other of that constantly.

Lisa Santivasci, wife

New York, Chicago, London, and most European cities. Pope John Paul declared that the Iraqi conflict "threatened the destiny of humanity."[4] For my own part, I was torn between driving out and trying to start a fight at a peace march, or sitting home alone and worrying about what Phil was about to encounter when he and his unit crossed into Iraq.

In his televised ultimatum to Saddam Hussein and his sons to leave Iraq within 48 hours, President Bush said, "Their refusal to do so will result in military conflict, commenced at a time of our own choosing . . . ."

At least now I had a date on which I could focus, in which the war would finally begin.

That time was 1230, on 21 March 2003, as the 55 men and six 155mm howitzers of Charlie Battery, carrying 228 years of balls-to-the wall Marine tradition, barreled through the berms on their way into Iraq.

Chapter 6

Battle of An Nasiriyah

These men on the line were my family, my home. They
were closer to me than I can say …. They had never
let me down, and I couldn't do it to them ….
Men, I now knew do not fight for flag or
country or glory … they fight
for one another.

William Manchester[5]

21 March–2 April 2003

Unlike his father with Operation Desert Storm in 1991, President George W. Bush launched his war with ground forces. While it would probably not be an exaggeration to say that at least half of the televisions in America were tuned to the bombs and rockets slamming into Baghdad, the truth was that the Marines and Army started the invasion by pouring across the border in huge mobile columns and began firing on the Iraqis hours before the start of the much-publicized air campaign.

This was a multi-faceted invasion plan, as America and the world would soon learn. The Army was to head for Baghdad by using an overland desert route, instead of the Iraqi highway system. At the same time, the 1st Marine Expeditionary Force (MEF) split into two parts, with the 1st Marine Division heading north to Baghdad through the valley between the Tigris and Euphrates rivers, while elements of the 2nd Marine Division—which included Task Force Tarawa, RCT-2, and Charlie Battery—were tasked to seize and control Nasiriyah and southern Iraq.

A smaller Marine contingent—the 15th Marine Expeditionary Unit (MEU)—was ordered to support our British allies, whose Royal Marines and Army's special parachute brigades were ordered to quickly capture and secure the seaports of Basra and Um Qasr, along with the Rumaila Oil Fields. The Rumaila fields are one of the largest collections of oil and gas fields in the world, and it was important to gain control of them quickly in order to prevent the repetition of the intentional sabotage and environmental disasters that occurred in Desert Storm.

At that time, of course, I knew none of this, and neither did any of the other parents or wives. With one television on MSNBC, and the other on CNN, I spent 21 and 22 March glued to the TV, hoping for any news or mention of the Marine ground campaign. At the same time, watching the B-52s take off from our English allies' airbases, and seeing the cruise missiles strike Baghdad, just served to increase my worries about my son.

Back home, much of America watched NBC and David Bloom on his "Bloommobile" as he sat on his M-88 tank recovery vehicle and narrated the Army's 3rd Infantry Division story as they raced for Baghdad. With his cameras trained on the sights and sounds of this huge column of vehicles and men (a collection of some 7,000 M1 Abrams tanks, Bradley fighting vehicles, 7-ton trucks, and supply vehicles), I tried to use this amazing live coverage of our troops at war to gauge what Phil and his fellow Marines were experiencing wherever they were in Iraq.

Because the war had finally started, I had trouble concentrating on business. When I was traveling, I would only eat in a restaurant that had MSNBC or CNN playing on a television screen. At work, I must have dialed up the MSN or Yahoo website about every seven minutes to see what might be happening. There was almost nothing on the news about the Marines, except some small articles on the 1st MEF going into Basra, and that wasn't nearly good enough. A friend of mine warned me about being uptight, "You've got to relax. Phil is a good Marine, and he'll do fine. You can't let this consume you." Easier said than done.

Other parents, wives, and children felt the same as me. "At first, Richard and I lived in front of the television," said Nancy Turcotte. "I just sat on my couch and cried. I couldn't concentrate on my job. Fortunately, my mother helped a lot; she had lost her fiancé in WWII. But my savior was my aunt, Irene Murphy. Aunt Irene's husband was a surgeon who had served with the 2nd Marine Division at Tarawa. (How ironic is that?) She was the only person who really understood what I was going through."

Day 1: Across the LoD into Iraq

Friday, 21 March 2003

None of the parents or wives knew that after crossing through the berms, Charlie Battery and the rest of 1/10 had formed into a "Desert Wedge" as they rolled into Iraq with RCT-2. Leading RCT-2 into battle was Company C, 2nd Light-Armored Reconnaissance (LARs), followed by 1/2 Infantry Battalion, and then it was 1st Lt. Shea leading Charlie Battery, at the head of 1/10 Artillery, with 3/2 Infantry Battalion following. Each battery was driving abreast of each other with their Main Command Post (CP), Tactical CP (TAC-CP), radar, and supply battalions directly behind them.

"There were shitloads of LAVs and AAVs on our flanks," Corporal Czombos said later. "We were the main convoy going north, and it was just fucking awesome. I was pretty excited that we were moving—we'd spent a month in Camp Shoup, so it was about fucking time we got rolling!"

The Marines of RCT-2 and Charlie Battery spent their first day of the war driving cross-country through the rocky Iraqi countryside. They kept their speeds down to perhaps 20 to 30 mph, as they purposely limited their speed in order to avoid road damage to the guns. Top Santivasci explained they were going cross-country because the Army's 3rd Infantry Division had been given movement priority since they were headed for Baghdad. He said their trucks and vehicles jammed the roads. "I heard later that the 507th [Jessica Lynch's army unit] was mixed in here someplace, but we beat them to Nasiriyah anyway."

As the Marines drove deeper into Iraq, they remained on high alert. "We kept our M16s pointed outboard," said Phil, "on Condition 1." Corporal Gault laughed when he recalled the drive into the Iraqi desert, "Yeah, we had a lot of puckered assholes on our truck, too!" The tension only heightened when the Marines had to stop and disembark from their vehicles for a gas attack. Even though it was a false alarm, it delayed the drive by over an hour as they regrouped and remounted. Doc Sanders admitted, "No one knew what to expect, or when we'd be attacked or get a fire mission."

> We were all very tense as we crossed the LoD, and not seeing any Iraqis just kept us more on edge.
>
> *LCpl. Phil Lubin*

In all, Charlie Battery and the convoy drove for eight hours over some extremely difficult and dangerous terrain. The battalion's advance parties arrived at their first firing positions, the Al-Luhays Oil Fields, at approximately 1700, and then the main body, including Phil and Charlie Battery, pulled into their bivouac at

2000 and settled in for the night. Phil told me they bunked in their 7-tons that evening and tried to sleep. The back of their 7-ton truck was cold, dirty, and full of sand, and every noise served to wake them from their fitful dozing. Nerves and tension were making for difficult sleeping conditions. Lance Corporal Jones confirmed what most Charlie Battery Marines were experiencing, "I know I didn't sleep worth a shit. Who knew what was going to happen, or when it all might start?"

Day 2: First Action!

Between the nervous energy generated from the combat they all expected to begin momentarily, along with the requirement to stand guard duty, most of the Marines slept little during that Friday night and into the early Saturday morning hours. Most of Charlie Battery simply slept fitfully in their trucks, and just stared out into the dark Iraqi night.

At 0330, Charlie Battery and 1st Battalion formed up again, and moved out into the desert. Rolling north and west during the day, they maintained their Desert Wedge formation as they drove roughly parallel to the main Pipeline Road. At midmorning, however, the battalion halted, and C Company LAR and 1st Battalion, 2nd Marines (infantry) took the lead in their drive through the desert.

First Combat Fire Mission

Suddenly, at 1130, the battalion broke formation and formed into firing positions north of the Jalibah Airfield, as the 1/10 Counter Battery Radar (CBR) Detachment observed and tracked a number of incoming mortar rounds being fired at them from nearby. "It was a Hip Shot, and a Red Rain mission," said LCpl. Lamb. "We'd practiced this a thousand times; we knew exactly what to do."

Phil, as the recorder, took the firing order from Lamb and bellowed it to his fellow Marines on Gun #1: "Battery, 2 rounds, special instructions, when ready, charge 6 white, lot Delta Whiskey, shell ICM, fuse VT, time 12, deflection ... quadrant ...." With these simple commands, practiced by the hour in the cold and rain of Fort Sill, and the dust and wind of the Udairi Training Range, Phil and his fellow Marines on Gun #1, along with his friends on Guns 2–6, went to war.

Thus, Charlie Battery, supported by Alpha Battery, received Task Force Tarawa's first combat fire order of Operation Iraqi

Saturday, 22 March 2003

I don't think anyone in Charlie Battery got much sleep. Guys would try to catch a quick nap as we sat in our fighting pits or in the trucks.

Cpl. Chris Gault

Freedom, and they quickly and successfully knocked out an Iraqi mortar platoon at a distance of approximately six miles. "It was about time we did something," said LCpl. Bechu. "We'd been driving for two fucking days, and I was desperate to get out and start shooting!" Phil told me later that at the time, he knew the mission was for real, but it still seemed like a live-fire field operation. It was only later that he finally was able to say to himself, "Damn! Now I'm a combat Marine!"

We drew the first Iraqi blood for Task Force Tarawa of the war!

LCpl. Joshua Jones

Later that same day, Charlie Battery and their fellow Marines of RCT-2 settled in for their second night since crossing the border. After 1st Lt. Shea and SSgt. Fontenoy sited the howitzers, the Marines dug their fighting pits and tried to get some rest. Brigadier General Richard Natonski of Task Force Tarawa issued orders for RCT-2 to move their forces north and slightly west towards Nasiriyah and to be ready to attack and seize the eastern bridges starting no later than 0700 local time. This was a verbal order issued sometime late afternoon 22 March.

By this time, the Marines were just foul with sand, dirt, and grime. While Camp Shoup had not been a holiday camp, it at least had minimal shower and water facilities; but after five days in the field, Phil and his friends were caked with the desert dirt and sand that stuck to them by perspiration and wind.

Phil and Cpl. Noyes joked a little about how bad they looked. "We had sand in our ears, in our eyes, and up our ass," Phil said. "We could cough up huge balls of snot any time we wanted to, and our lips were chapped and bloody from the dryness and the sand. Only a few of us had gotten packages from home, and we'd run out of chapstick and baby wipes a long time back." Noyes described how the blisters from their gas masks had callused over and they smelled bad to boot. He noted, "There wasn't a lot of toilet paper either."

Settling in for the night did not bring much sleep. Even those Marines not on watch mostly stayed awake. Since rolling across the LoD two days earlier, they'd only completed one Red Rain mission, but they sensed and knew more of the same was to come. Despite the exhaustion, they simply couldn't sleep. "I was just fucking exhausted," said Cpl. Czombos, "but I was still too wide awake to sleep. I guess I just didn't know what to do, so I just stayed awake and looked out most of the night, and worried about the next day."

Day 3: Welcome to Nasiriyah

Charlie Battery had no idea what the day would bring as they broke camp very early that morning. Operating on nervous energy, bad coffee, and months of desert training, the other Marines saddled up and were moving north on Highway 7, the road to Nasiriyah by 0130. "I had MRE-quality instant coffee mixed with cold water and sand, along with some candy," said Cpl. Jones, "and let me tell you, it wasn't very good." But it was sufficient to get them up and moving, and with 1st Lt. Shea's advance party leading the way, Phil and the others drove slowly in the dark stuck in an enormous traffic jam of Army vehicles all moving towards Nasiriyah.

Sunday, 23 March 2003

Why Nasiriyah Was Important

Control of Nasiriyah was important to the Marine and Coalition plan to take Baghdad quickly. As a result, RCT-2 was tasked to seize the eastern bridges of the city spanning the Euphrates River and Saddam Canal. By securing these choke-points over the Euphrates River and the Saddam Canal, the Marines would thereby control access into and through the city.

While the Army initially detoured around the city in their race north, the Marines needed to control the city in order to secure the bridges so the all-important supply convoys kept rolling. Since it takes five gallons of gas just to start an M1 Abrams tank, one can just imagine the huge amount of food and fuel needed to supply the Marine and Army units on their dash to Baghdad. Additionally, because of the necessity to keep the troops and vehicles well supplied, control of the nearby Tallil Airbase was equally valuable; American and British cargo planes could land there and keep the forward troops re-supplied. In all, Nasiriyah was a city that had to be taken, and taken quickly.

Therefore, on Saturday night, 21 March 2003, the Marines of RCT-2 were on the move to Nasiriyah having been told to be ready to enter the city in order to take control of the bridges and the routes running through it.

As RCT-2 drew closer to the city, they were led by 1/2's infantry, closely followed by 1st Lt. Shea and 1/10's 18 howitzers. Commanded by Lt. Col. Rick Grabowski, 1/2 pulled into their planned position at the 20 Northing (a phase line on the map) at 0551 local time, an hour ahead of the planned schedule. Grabowski's infantry was told to "be prepared to" attack and seize two key bridge crossings; the south bridge over the Euphrates River, and a second bridge some two miles further north that spanned the Saddam Canal.

RCT-2's plan was that after 1/2 seized the eastern bridges, the "follow-on" units would clear and control Highway 8 (or the "Q Route") up through the eastern side of Nasiriyah. The follow-on units were the infantry of 2/8, commanded by Lt. Col. Royal Mortenson, and then the infantry of 3/2, led by Lt. Col. Paul Dunahoe.

The Q Route became commonly known as "Ambush Alley" because it was an open and exposed stretch of road stretching some four kilometers through the city between the eastern bridges over the Euphrates and the northern bridge over the Saddam Canal. The Q Route eventually connected with Highway 7, which was north-west of Nasiriyah and the main road route to Baghdad. So the sooner 1/2 secured the bridges, and 2/8 and 3/2 could maintain bridge and route security, the sooner 1st MEF could concentrate on moving combat units from 1st Marine Division through Nasiriyah up the Q Route and push north up Highway 7 for the upcoming battle to take Baghdad.

Marine Corps routes into Iraq from Kuwait

A Very Serious Miscalculation

Both Pentagon Intelligence and various administration figures, such as Paul Wolfowitz, had blithely declared that since Nasiriyah was a Shiite city (the competing Moslem group who had suffered so terribly under the Sunni regime of Saddam Hussein), the Marines and Allied troops would be welcomed into the city as conquering heroes. The prevailing thinking was that the Marines would find limited, if not half-hearted, resistance.

This type of thinking was so prevalent that Lt. Colonels Grabowski, Dunahoe, and Mortenson all recounted stories where they were told by Coalition Intelligence that their men might well be met by crowds of cheering Shiites, rather than fanatical defenders.

Senior military planners could not have been more wrong in their assumptions. The Iraqi defenders were commanded by General Ali Hassan Al-Majid, one of Saddam Hussein's most ruthless relatives. Al-Majid commanded both the Baa'thist regular army, as well as the younger Fedayeen contingent, and by looking at any map of Nasiriyah, the Iraqi defenders knew exactly what route the Marines had to take through the city.

Even as recently as the prior day, Army Intelligence had reported to the Marines that Nasiriyah was clear. Since Nasiriyah was Shiite, and therefore assumed to be a friendly city, neither the MEB or MEF provided any unmanned drone flights over the city. At this point, no one in either Task Force Tarawa or RCT-2 headquarters had any idea of who, where, or if there was any Iraqi opposition in the city.

The repercussion of Army Intelligence denying Lt. Col. Grabowski's request for surveillance was that the Marines of RCT-2 were completely unaware that the Iraqi Army was in Nasiriyah in force. In fact, Army Intelligence had reported only the day before that the Iraqi 11th Infantry Division in Nasiriyah would not fight.

In reality, however, the Iraqis had set an ambush on the south side of the city which included tanks, artillery, mortars, and a substantial body of troops. These Iraq troops consisted both of regular army soldiers from their 11th Infantry Division, the 51st Mechanized Infantry Division, as well as the less-disciplined, but far more motivated, Fedayeen paramilitary and guerrilla forces such as the Saddam Fedayeen and the Al-Quds. Hence, the lead elements, and therefore the most exposed Marine units—those of Charlie Battery and 1/10, who were following directly behind Lt. Col. Grabowski's infantry companies in 1/2—were completely unaware of the Iraqi intent to aggressively defend their city.

Originally from Farmington, Iowa, Lt. Col. Grabowski was a career Marine who had served in 1994's Operation Uphold Democracy. As the operations officer for 2nd Battalion, 2nd Marine Regiment, his battalion had engaged and killed twelve Haitian military police in a firefight in Port-Au-Prince, so he was no stranger to the specific problems inherent in city combat. He was understandably leery about sending his men into an area without knowledge of either his opponents or even the terrain, and therefore, he had ordered his lead company to advance carefully into the city.

But as the lead elements of 1/2 Marines arrived at their holding positions in preparation for their drive into Nasiriyah, they began taking both indirect and direct fire at approximately 0600 (local Iraqi time). The Iraqi troops were firing on the Marines from both sides of the Q Route from camouflaged machine gun nests, mortar batteries, as well as dug-in tanks, hull-down.

"Because we didn't expect to fight," said SSgt. Fontenoy, "we didn't shape the battlefield. By that, I mean we shell the area that we're about to attack with the goal of destroying any forces that might oppose us. But since we were supposed to just roll through the town, and we had been told it was friendly, we weren't ordered to do any prep work. And that hurt us; we went right into combat cold, with the Iraqis untouched."

The howitzers and Marines of Charlie Battery were still some 20 kilometers (12.4 miles) from advancing into the city when the gunfight broke out. Suddenly, the Marine Command had to re-evaluate the potential resistance within the city, except that they had no hard data or intelligence from which to work. "It was too late to shape the battlefield," Gunny Lambert explained. "We'd thought the city was friendly, so we didn't shell it."

And now, they had a battle on their hands.

Alpha and Bravo batteries were therefore immediately called forward to support their fellow Marines, and they raced forward and set "Hasty Emplacements." Bravo Battery was ready to fire first, and immediately received a Red Rain mission against a battery of Iraqi 105mm howitzers. With two volleys of DPICMs (Dual Purpose Improved Conventional Munitions), Bravo Battery successfully destroyed the Iraqi artillery at 0710 local time, completing the first fire mission of what was to become known as the Battle of An Nasiriyah.

The 507th Blunder

As this fighting was beginning to unfold, another (unrelated) action was taking place nearby; an action that would quickly lead to an escalation of both the battle and the war.

Earlier that morning, (at approximately 0430 local time), an Army convoy blundered into the city well ahead of the advancing

---

Our AP began to set up our initial gun position at 0630. We were to support 1/2's Infantry as they went forward to seize the eastern bridges.

1st Lt. Sean Shea

Because we didn't expect to fight, we didn't prep the battlefield.

SSgt. John Fontenoy

Marines. This was the Army's 507th of Jessica Lynch fame, and they were lost and late. After only two days, they were already some 20 hours behind their main body, and as they drove through the Iraqi desert with their headlights lights still blazing, a huge dust cloud trailed behind them.

Charlie Battery's advance party of 1st Lt. Shea, SSgt. Fontenoy, and LCpl. Goodson were just about to drive north up to Nasiriyah, as this unidentified convoy tooled through the desert. These Marines, along with Phil, Noyes, Gault, and a few others, watched as the trucks turned onto the Q Route and went due north directly into the city.

"Who was that?" SSgt. Fontenoy wondered out loud. "We have no convoys rolling ahead of us."

Whoever they were, they were "hauling ass" as Phil remembers. "They came trucking past us with their lights on. No one had any idea who they were."

Approximately 90 minutes later, one truck reappeared out of the city, changing directions several times, as if the driver could not decide where the American lines were. After approximately 15 minutes, the unidentified truck finally headed for the safety of the Marines' front lines.

It was the sole survivor of the Army's 507th Maintenance Company, who had taken Highway 8 into Nasiriyah, driven up the Q Route through the city and then out the northern end to Highway 7, where they finally realized their mistake, turned around, and drove back SOUTH through the city a second time, in an attempt to exit Nasiriyah. But the Iraqis reacted the second time the 507th drove past them, and their dug-in tanks, mortars, and troops riddled the unprepared and ill-trained Army maintenance group.

"This unknown truck arrived at my lead company (Team Tank), who was already under enemy fire," Lt. Col. Grabowski recalled. "Team Tank's commander, Major Bill Peeples, reported to me that he'd rescued 3–4 in the first truck, most of them wounded, along with their unit commander. Their commander told us that he had more soldiers stranded some 4–5 klicks north, up Highway 8, so I authorized Major Peeples to move forward, and he eventually recovered eleven additional soldiers, four of whom were wounded.

Marines rescue the Army's 507th

It was shortly after the Marines' first rescue of the 507th that General Natonski came up to the front lines personally, and ordered Lt. Col. Grabowski to send his Marines forward and attack and seize the two eastern bridges of Nasiriyah.

Unexpected and Fierce Opposition

The Marines suddenly realized they were in a serious fight as the Iraqis, emboldened by their success in destroying the 507th so easily, began attacking the Marine infantry from both sides of the highway. As the Marines of 1/2 readied themselves to move forward to seize the two key bridges, the Iraqis began firing on the infantry from the houses and sheltered positions from both sides of the road.

Top Santivasci remembered it all too well. "They had 'dug-in' tanks, mortars, arty, 37mm anti-aircraft guns, as well as two trench lines of troops. They were waiting for us, but the 507th got hit instead. We would have been hit hard—we had no idea they were there." As a result, what was expected to be a simple task of being ready to potentially provide support for the Marines of 1/2 suddenly became much more difficult and intense for Phil, Charlie Battery, and the other cannoneers of 1/10.

> The Intel we had was very misleading, and things got harder than we expected.
>
> *GySgt. Clay Lambert*

Intelligence Fails the Marines Again

After the M1 Abrams Marine 8th tanks moved up to help recover the wounded survivors of the 507th, two of Lt. Col. Grabowski's infantry companies (Alpha and Bravo) began to roll up into the city. Suddenly, they discovered a railroad overpass that was not featured on the map. This overpass was only about four kilometers south from the Euphrates River Bridge. Defending the bridge, in a line east to west of the overpass, were nine Iraqi T-55 battle tanks; yet another distressing surprise for the Marines who discovered that not only were they fighting against Iraqi soldiers, but they were facing these nine tanks, as well as Iraqi mortars and artillery. They promptly called back to Lt. Col. Starnes and his men for artillery support.

As the infantry from 1/2 engaged the Iraqi tanks at the railroad overpass, Charlie Battery was rushed forward up Highway 7, forward of Bravo and Alpha batteries, in order to provide artillery support for their grunts. "We got the guns sited as quick as we could," said Phil. "I could hear the gun fight up ahead of us, and you couldn't miss the huge plumes of smoke from the burning trucks. I knew that this was going to be a lot harder than when we took out the mortar battery the day before."

With the Marines of 1/2 now past the railroad overpass, and getting ready to advance across the Euphrates River Bridge and into the city, Phil and Charlie Battery entered the battle. "We were receiving fire missions as we were siting our gun," Phil said later, "and then we just shot all day long." Turcotte remembered it the same way. "I had no track of time; all we did was re-site the gun and shoot." In fact, they were shelling enemy positions in the southern sector of the city, in direct support of their 1/2 Marine brothers.

As a result of rescuing the 507th, Lt. Col. Grabowski's tank company was low on fuel and had to begin refueling operations. Bravo Company, therefore, took the lead in assaulting the city, and requested anti-armor support. Their Combined Anti-Armor Team (CAAT) began engaging the Iraqi tanks with their TOW and Javelin anti-tank missiles, and in conjunction with 1/10's artillery fire, the Iraqi tanks were quickly destroyed. "We fired missions all morning," said Phil. "We knew things were bad by the amount we were shooting."

As the sun continued to rise, the battalion began to leapfrog its units north in order to get closer to the city and support the infantry. The three batteries were given fire for effect (FFE) and adjust fire (AF) missions, as their forward observers (FOs) worked hard to keep Charlie Battery and the others firing in full support of 1/2 and 2/8. Charlie Battery and the others had already shot some 108 DPICM rounds, and it was just reaching 0900.

Now, however, the battle turned as ugly for 1/10's cannoneers as it was turning for the 1/2's infantry. At 0945, as Bravo Battery's AP readied itself to again move forward, the main body began to receive severe and heavy mortar fire, which forced the Bravo's CO, Captain Brian Sharp, to order them to conduct an emergency displacement, and moved back in order to rejoin the main group.

Finally, a platoon of four M1 Abrams tanks were now refueled, and they came rumbling north up Highway 7, across the railroad overpass. The tankers met up with the infantry, who were taking serious incoming fire as they huddled south of the Euphrates River Bridge. With the arrival of the tanks, Lt. Col. Grabowski reorganized his Marines as "Team Mech" (as in "mechanized"); a combined group of tanks and infantry mounted in the AAVs.

Moving Closer to the Bridges

With this armored help, the Marine infantry began to break through the Iraqi defense and force their way deeper into the city closer to the bridges, and the infantry FOs were finally able to identify Iraqi targets within the city. Charlie Battery and the other batteries fired on—and destroyed—machine gun bunkers, two of the nine T-62 tanks, as well as entrenched Iraqi infantry. They fired a variety of missions, ranging from Immediate Suppression (IS) to Fire For Effect (FFE).

As the Marine infantry companies advanced across the Euphrates River Bridge, they began taking fire from the Iraqi defenders. The volume of fire increased in both volume and noise, as the Marines begin seeking shelter from the incoming RPGs, small arms, and heavy machine gun fire. Even those Marines inside the AAVs were still vulnerable, as their AAVs are made of the soft-sided aluminum variety, compared to the enhanced armored AAVs used by the 1st MEF.

The Plan of Attack

Sometime around 1030–1100, Bravo Company (1/2) was ordered to move forward and lead the battalions' attack into the city. Charlie Company was moved up on Bravo's left flank to provide security. Alpha Company was to follow in trace of Bravo Company thus forming a classic two-up and one back mechanized maneuver. It was anticipated that as the two lead companies approached the Euphrates River, the terrain would become more restrictive and therefore require Charlie Company to fall back and in trace of Alpha Company. Bravo Company would seize the Euphrates River Bridge and if enemy resistance was light would rapidly envelope east of the city in an effort to avoid the urban build-up and establish a support by fire position east of the Saddam Canal Bridge.

Following behind the lead assault unit, Alpha Company was tasked to occupy and secure the Euphrates River Bridge and fan out to maintain bridge security. Once this was accomplished, Charlie Company would pass through Alpha's positions and continue east of the city with the final mission to by-pass Bravo Company and seize the Saddam Canal Bridge.

The plan was risky, but if it worked, the Marines of 1/2 would seize both bridges while avoiding a four-kilometer stretch of highway nicknamed by Army planners as Ambush Alley. Once the bridges were seized, follow-on units from RCT-2 would secure the transit route through Nasiriyah without the fighting and losses normally incurred in city fighting. The ugly American losses suffered in the October 1993 "Blackhawk Down" Battle in Mogadishu was very much on the minds of the Marine commanders.

The Mud & Muck Factor

But when Bravo Company came off the bridge and swung right as ordered, the battle plan partially unraveled as they immediately bogged down in a thick mud that immobilized their M1 Abrams tanks, their many AAVs, as well as additional tanks (and an M88 Tank Retriever sent to free them from the glop). At this point, the Iraqis set upon the Marines in the city with a fury, and the battle increased in ferocity.

Back several miles in their own sector of the battlefield, Top Santivasci, SSgt. Fontenoy, LCpl. Turcotte, LCpl. Bechu and Phil, and the other Marines had the same problem. As they pulled off the highway to site their guns and begin to fire, they were caught in the same type of crusted-over ooze that had trapped Bravo Company. Even the ground beneath the Marines began to betray them, and many of their Humvees and other vehicles began to break through the solid-looking sand and bog down in mud and muck underneath. "Driving suddenly was an absolute bitch," said Cpl. Goodson. "We were in an area where it looked okay, but actually, it was some sort of crust, and so I got us stuck in the mud. I was yelling at Aguila to stay alert, but Lieutenant Shea told us to stay calm."

1/10's First Casualty

As the three infantry companies fought to free their vehicles (and at the same time defend themselves from their Iraqi attackers), the Bravo Company Commander told his XO to take one platoon and provide security around the stuck vehicles while the rest of Bravo continued its movement north to the Saddam Canal in order to establish a support-by-fire position. Bravo Company was the only unit to have stuck vehicles. Regrettably, Bravo was unable to reach the Saddam Canal due to the city fighting in which they were now involved. This one platoon provided security for the stuck vehicles while 1/2's recovery effort was taking place. Later, they linked up with Bravo Company just prior to moving north of the city.

Charlie Company shot across the Saddam Canal Bridge in their AAVs, and without warning, found themselves in the midst

Marines of gun #5, L to R: Cpl. Michael Czombos, Cpl. Brandon Barton, LCpl. Brandon Bobko, Cpl. Kenneth Palsiance, Cpl. Thomas Albee, Cpl. Jorge Delarosa, Cpl. Mike VanValkenburg, Sgt. Robert Banfield

Hurry up, goddamn it! We've got Marines dying up there!

Sgt. Robert Banfield

of an Iraqi preplanned engagement area. As the company came off the bridge, they found themselves in open terrain which was being aggressively defended by members of the Iraqi 2nd Battalion/ 23rd Infantry Brigade. "All hell broke loose here," recalled Lt. Col. Grabowski, "as the Iraqis engaged my men with 105mm howitzers, mortars, 57mm recoilless rifles, RPGs, as well as intense small arms fire."

At about the same time, in the now-famous radio call back for assistance, Top Santivasci and the others back in the CP heard that the Marines of 1/2 on the northern bridge were calling back for artillery support. "Timberwolf is taking fire!"

Not only did they need immediate support, but they had one of 1/10's Marines, 1st Lt. Fred Pokorney, up on the bridge with them. He was 1/10's FO and had been sent forward with 1/2 to call fire missions back to 1/10's battery FDCs.

As the Iraqi barrage slammed into the Marines, Charlie Company dismounted their AAVs and broke for cover in order to return fire. First Lieutenant Pokorney ran some 300 yards north along the highway, seeking cover with two other Marines in order to call in artillery support. He was able to call in two fire missions, and was in the process of calling in a third, when his position was struck by Iraqi RPGs. He and two of 1/2's Marines were killed. First Lieutenant Pokorney, who hailed from Tonopah, Nevada, was 1/10's first casualty in the war, and he left behind a wife, Carolyn Rochelle, and a two-year-old daughter, Taylor. He was respected and liked by all as both a man and a Marine.

An Artillery "Nightmare"

1st Battalion, Tenth Marines (1/10) calls itself "First in the World" as in the world's best artillery battalion. With a call sign of "Nightmare," which was indicative of what they were about to inflict on the Iraqis opposing them, Lt. Col. Starnes' artillery batteries—made up of young Marines like Phil and the others in their first war—began to prove their expertise that morning. As the FOs began to locate targets and call them back to the TAC-CP, Gunny Lambert's training took over in the heat and fatigue of battle, and the Charlie Battery Marines loaded and fired in a constant nonstop whirl of smoke and noise. "I walked the gun line a lot the first day," said Gunny Lambert. "I figured the boys would be a little nervous, this being their first combat and all, so I went around to check them out. They were all a little shaky, so I reminded them that this was no worse than my training ops, and that they were doing fine."

"We didn't stop firing," Phil remembered later. "It seemed that we shot missions nonstop, and that we didn't let up the whole time. When I had a chance to look up, I could see our Cobras flying up, and then hovering and firing at targets down in the city. They'd empty their whole ammo load, and sometimes you could see their spent brass just raining down from where they were firing."

Corporal Noyes remembered that when he had the time to look out into the battlefield, all he saw were 7-ton trucks full of Marines moving up, and the wounded Marines being hustled back for treatment and evacuation. "I didn't know what to expect," he said, "but it sure seemed that suddenly this wasn't such a friendly city!"

With his previous combat experience from Desert Storm, Lt. Shea was able to maintain a perspective different than that of most of his younger Marines. "The sergeants on the gun line—Sgt. Peter Peterson, Sgt. Adam Wald, and Sgt. Robert Banfield—all conducted themselves in exemplary fashion. During the battle, I was privileged to watch their focus, determination, and relentless drive to accomplish their mission and punish our enemy. And on our flanks, on Guns 1 and 6, SSgt. John Twiggs and SSgt. Bolton were equally awesome."

The Iraqis weren't just rolling over this time.

Cpl. Justin Noyes

Not only were Iraqis not rolling over for the Marines, but in fact, the battle only got more vicious for both the Marine infantry and the cannoneers. Another frustration for the Marine Command was the trouble they were experiencing helping out their infantry. Top Santivasci commented later that part of the problem was the FOs were under Iraqi fire and that the FDC controllers couldn't communicate effectively with them. Then to make matters worse, the entire radio network went down. Consequently, they couldn't help the infantry with their artillery support. Santivasci said, "You can't just wildly shell the city, we could have hit our Marines."

I was most scared when I saw the dead and wounded Marines being brought back through our lines. It was them; it could easily be me.

Cpl. Michael Czombos

While communications remained problematic during the first few days of the battle, the first day was the worst. Assistance, however, came from a most welcomed corner.

British Reinforcements

Reinforcements were already on the scene. A 105mm light gun battery and "Arthur" radar unit of England's famed 16th Air Assault Brigade had seemingly materialized out of the desert dust and offered their assistance to 1/10. G Parachute Battery (Mercer's Troop) Royal Horse Artillery was commanded by Captain Gibson Barclay, and they had been moving north and west by vehicle in order to support an airborne assault of the Qulat Sukkar Airfield, some 35 miles north of Nasiriyah, by the 1st PARA Battlegroup.

They had been driving from the Basra area of operations on Route Tampa. "Your Marine convoys were huge," said Battery G Sgt. David Pearce, "and the roads were blocked for miles." Upon getting close to the city, and finding the road through Nasiriyah to Qulat Sukkar blocked because of the battle, Captain Barclay and his men volunteered their services (and their guns) to RCT-2. The offer was gratefully accepted, and the men of Battery G eagerly set up along their American artillery brothers and joined the battle.

"We set up our gun line to the right of Highway 7," said Sgt. Paul Dickinson, "and when Dave and I set up our CP, we got involved in the action immediately." Both the Marines and the British troops used a laptop computer-like device called the "Blue Force Tracker," which superimposes friendly and enemy locations over a map grid. "As we got set up, Sgt. Billy Morris saw a mass of red dots slam into a smaller group of blue dots, and he got on the radio and asked, 'Are you all right?' Well, they replied that they couldn't get thru to their CP, and could we relay their fire missions? Too right we could! Billy spent the morning helping pass the fire missions from your Marines up on the Saddam Canal back to your FDCs!"

Battery G established their positions only some 600 meters south of the city limits and were thus the Allied unit closest to the city. Having already had the "honour" of being the

Sgt. Billy Moore (left) and Sgt. David Pearce of UK Battery G

first British unit to fire during the opening days of the war, they proved even more invaluable as they added both their guns and their radar unit to the Marines.

In addition, 1/10's three artillery batteries were reinforced by an artillery battery from the 1st MEF, the 1/11. While Task Force Tarawa Command did not yet know if they needed to leave the unit here, or could take it north to Baghdad, RCT-2 used 1/11's firepower—as well as its ammunition—in the fight to take Nasiriyah. With 1/11 and the UK's Battery G added to the emplaced and blooded Marines of 1/10, there were now 42 heavy guns shelling Nasiriyah.

Behind them and to the left, and with their world consisting solely and simply of completing their fire missions, Phil and Bechu on Gun 1, Gallagher and Jones on Guns 2 and 3, and Czombos and Noyes on Guns 5 and 6 could only begin to guess how difficult the battle was becoming for the Marines this first day in An Nasiriyah.

Battle Recap: Early Afternoon

By early afternoon on Sunday, 23 March 2003, the battle to secure the routes through Nasiriyah was evolving into exactly the type of battle the Marines had tried to avoid.

> Charlie Company 1/2 was fighting for their lives three klicks north up Ambush Alley, across the Saddam Canal Bridge, and had suffered both KIAs and WIAs.
>
> Bravo Company 1/2 was still fighting their way out of the muck across and to the right of the Euphrates River Bridge.
>
> Alpha Company 1/2 was fanned out around the northern end of the Euphrates River Bridge and fighting off the Iraqi Fedayeen defenders.
>
> Behind them, Lt. Col. Mortenson's 2/8 Infantry was called forward to cross the Euphrates River Bridge in order to conduct a relief in place with Alpha Company 1/2.
>
> Lt. Col. Dunahoe's men of 3/2 were hustled down from the western side of An Nasiriyah to provide support for 2/8.

And through all this, in response to the repeated frantic calls for help from their infantrymen, the cannoneers of 1/10's Charlie,

Bravo, and Alpha batteries were simply shelling the shit out of the city as quickly and as accurately as possible.

It was through these hours of confusion, exhaustion, noise, and battle in which Phil, Bechu, Jones, and all the young Charlie Battery Marines became combat veterans. "While it took us commanders longer than we liked to get a sense of the battle," Lt. Col. Grabowski explained later, "it didn't take Colonel Starnes' artillerymen or my infantry any time at all to adjust. All these young Marines just performed wonderfully."

The Marine After-Action Report for the day describes how well Charlie, Bravo, and Alpha batteries performed under the pressure of battle: "The Battalion prosecuted missions with a speed unparalleled in training environments. Not only were these missions timely, but extraordinarily accurate."[6]

Ambush Alley

1/10's firing needed to both be accurate and timely as they were protecting their fellow Marines who were fighting their way through Ambush Alley (or the Q Route), the major route through Nasiriyah. Ambush Alley was an open and exposed stretch of road and necessary for taking the eastern and northern bridges. Despite the concerted effort of Infantry 1/2, 2/8, and 3/2, the Marines were fighting both entrenched and mobile Iraqi armor and the fighting had degenerated to door-to-door and from across the roads. The Iraqi defenders were primarily shooting from houses that were set back 25–75 yards off the highway, and the young Marines had to either destroy the houses or dig out the Iraqis house-by-house.

This was war on a rifle team level—our 18- to 20-year-old Marines against their Fedayeen.

Lt. Col. Rick Grabowski

Trying to Follow the War on the Homefront

Meanwhile, no one back home knew any of this. Despite the presence of the embedded reporters, most of the television news was focused on the Army's 101st as David Bloom on his M88 tank retriever narrated his exciting "Race to Baghdad." Late that night, however, the war changed in both tone and intensity for us parents and spouses as the violence and confusion of our sons' and husbands' battle in Nasiriyah was aired for the world to see.

Suddenly, I was wide awake. MSNBC was playing on my television, as usual, and it was approximately 0235 EST, Sunday morning, 23 March 2003, as I watched the following scene unfold on my TV screen:

Ken Kalthoff of NBC Fort Worth was reporting live from Iraq, lying in the sand, the camera on him shaking as Marine artillery was screaming just overhead. He was shouting into the camera about the "relentless Marine artillery fire from just behind him . . . firing for hours . . . all coming from 2nd Marine Division 1/10."

"Jesus Christ! That's Phil's unit!" I was instantly out of bed, standing in front of the TV, just yelling for Phil and his friends to keep it up. I shouted to them through the TV, "Keep it going, and just fuck them up good!"

It's a very odd feeling to see your son's unit fighting live on TV—an absolutely helpless, useless feeling. I felt I shouldn't be where I was; I should be there next to my son, helping him.

While some of us sat in front of any operable TV that had any war news on it, others could not watch it at all. Jamie Lambert, Gunny's wife, was one of the latter. "I just couldn't bear to watch the TV," she said. "It was my responsibility to be strong for my wives, and for my son, so I had to be extra careful to be sure I kept my composure." Laura Doggett, LCpl. Sobola Bechu's girlfriend, had the same problem with the TV news as did Mrs. Lambert. "I couldn't watch it on the TV; in fact, I avoided it. Except I checked casualty figures and names in the newspapers every day, so I knew Sobola was still alive."

Christy Fontenoy had similar problems with following the war on TV. "Cody and I sat on the couch and watched the war on TV, and then after he went to bed, I just sat there all night and watched it again. But then one day, he told me he was having nightmares about his dad dying, so I realized it was time to keep the TVs off."

Lisa Santivasci, who had missed Ken Kalthoff's NBC report that night, said later that she thought it was probably just as well. "I couldn't watch TV, but I couldn't sleep. I heard every car door open and shut on the entire street, and I'd jump out of my skin. I imagined it was the Marine Corps coming to tell me about my husband."

This anxiety only intensified during those stressful days as TV news reports repeatedly mentioned how a group of Iraqi soldiers brandishing a white flag had approached a Marine amphibious assault vehicle (from 1/2), as if to surrender, but when the Marines came closer, the Iraqis destroyed their AAV with an RPG round, killing six Marines. While I did not know if this particular story was true or not, my fear was that if Nasiriyah was the Pentagon's idea of a friendly city, I could not begin to imagine

> My husband would make me turn off the TV. We were totally mesmerized by the war news.
>
> *Nancy Turcotte, mother*

> Every dead or injured Marine or soldier I saw on the TV looked exactly like Michael.
>
> *Lisa Santivasci, wife*

what Phil would encounter as he and the others drew closer to Baghdad.

Like the families back home, the Marines had also heard about the Iraqis who had pretended to surrender and then killed our Marines the day before. Phil recalled how he and his gun crew had talked about the incident and "We decided that we'd do what we could to get even."

At Day's End

By the end of this first day of combat in Nasiriyah, the Marines of 1/10 had done a good job of getting even. Their howitzers had destroyed five tanks, a D30 battery, as well as conducted several Red Rain missions that destroyed an Iraqi artillery unit shelling 1/2 Infantry. Additionally, they fired a mission that screened another Alpha Company 1/2 during its movements through the city.

Back in the United States that night on AltaVista, and then in *The New York Times* the next day (23 March), I read and re-read Michael Wilson's short article about Task Force Tarawa's Red Rain action titled, "At Desert Airfield, Artillery Unit encounters 'Red Rain'." The sterility of the article did not seem to jibe with the brief, but intense mention on MSNBC of how ferociously the Battle of Nasiriyah was actually being fought, and so I sat there without a clue as what my son and his unit was encountering in their first day of combat.

But at the same time back in Nasiriyah, Top Santivasci, Gunny Lambert, and other senior NCOs knew exactly what they'd encountered. The Iraqis were fighting back, and surprisingly effectively. The Marines of RCT-2 had taken casualties: 1/10 lost 1st Lt. Pokorney; 1/2 suffered Marines killed and wounded; and 2/8 had wounded Marines also. The last bridge over the Saddam Canal was considered secured between 1400 and 1430 (local time), and by the end of the day, 1/2 had consolidated its positions north of the city and was making preparations to expand its position beyond the forced bridgehead on this northern bridge. 1st MEF was now able to run their troops and trucks up the Q Route and on to Baghdad—but just barely.

Day 4: Combat Continues in Nasiriyah

Monday, 24 March 2003

Although the two sets of bridges had been secured the evening before, and the 1st MEF convoys could tenuously move north, the Fedayeen attacks on the convoys continued. All it would take was a successful RPG attack on a convoy, and the Q Route could become a deathtrap for any of the Marines in the 7-tons who might be caught in it. The situation was precarious, and both the attacking Marines and the Iraqi defenders knew it.

Phil and his friends on Gun #1, along with his friends on the other five guns of Charlie Battery, were moving and firing through the chilly desert night. As the sun rose that Monday morning, they and the battalion remained heavily engaged against their Iraqi opposition, as they moved north on Highway 8 and began to close in on the city. They continued to fire in support of their 1/2 Infantry, who had moved up Highway 7 past the Saddam Canal, north of the city, as well as the motorized battalions of 3/2 and 2/8, who were fighting in the southern section of the city. The Iraqis were bringing in their reinforcements by truck, by bus, and even by taxi, and they showed no sign or interest in surrendering their city.

By midmorning, the three batteries had moved to within five kilometers of the city. Bravo Battery was farthest north, located to the west of Highway 8. Alpha Battery was several hundred yards south, to the east of the highway, and Charlie Battery was slightly further to the south. "We were arrayed in a 'V' formation," Phil explained, "with the TAC-CP being slightly forward of us."

With Bravo and Alpha so exposed, the engineers began to berm-in Charlie's six guns. With Charlie relatively secured, they began providing security for the Main CP. Phil, Hebert, Warren and the others on Gun #1; Gallagher and Barr on Gun #2; Jones and Gault on #3; Delarosa and Czombos on #5, and all the rest of the battery continued to work hard keeping the Iraqis at bay.

Staff Sergeant Fontenoy was busy too. "As the security chief for the battery," he said, "I'm responsible for the defense of the gun line. It was my responsibility to site our crew-served weapons on the berms. I mapped out the quadrants, and then set up and arranged the personnel to man the weapons when necessary." Fontenoy went on to explain that setting up and manning the crew-served weapons was very unusual for an artillery battery. Normally, an artillery battery fires on an enemy anywhere from 5 to 20 miles away. But in the Battle at Nasiriyah, the Iraqis were often less than a mile away, and at times, Alpha and Charlie batteries were firing at virtually point-blank range with their barrels lowered to almost horizontal.

Nasiriyah was for sure the real deal!

SSgt. John Fontenoy

The FOs called their "targets of opportunity" back to LCpl. Lamb and the other FDCs, and the Battalion CP processed and approved the fire missions constantly. All the weeks of practice and aggravation in the desert came together that morning, as Charlie, Alpha, and Bravo batteries conducted numerous "out-of-traverse" missions. Now they understood the reasons for the hours of dropping the skid plates and humping their 155s around to different targets, as they consistently shifted their gun and fired within three minutes of receiving their mission details.

The hours of practice at the Udairi Training Range under Gunny Lambert's baleful watch, where he emphasized speed and harangued them for accuracy, all melded together in the smoke and fire of the morning's excitement and confusion of battle. Later, Charlie Battery and the other two batteries received repeated compliments, including those of Col. Ronald Bailey, RCT-2's commanding officer, who later wrote that "In 25 years, he had never witnessed such responsive and accurate fire."[7]

Steady Stream of Civilians

During the early afternoon, at approximately 1240, a Marine sapper (engineering) battalion destroyed a huge Iraqi munitions cache in the southern section of Nasiriyah. Not surprisingly, many residents of Nasiriyah took this massive explosion as an excellent reason to leave the city, and soon, a steady stream of Iraqi civilians headed south-bound. For the remaining eight days of the battle, the batteries had to contend with Iraqi civilians walking through their positions as they continued to fire on their Iraqi Army targets. "It was nuts," Phil said. "Here we were, firing our 155, and absolutely blasting the city, we've got Marines on the berms guarding us and watching for Iraqis, and all these kids and women and families kept flowing towards us, and then past us."

Perfection Under Pressure

At the same time that Grabowski's Marines were trying to clear Ambush Alley so the 1st MEF convoy's could safely roll north, Charlie, Bravo and Alpha batteries, as well as UK Battery G, put on an incredible display of artillery firing to support their fellow Marines. Firing repeated Code Red missions, these missions (similar to a rolling barrage) had to be perfectly timed to support the Marine convoys racing through the city at 60 mph. In order to protect their fellow Marines, Charlie Battery had to drop their rounds only 300 meters in front of the supply and troop convoys barreling through Nasiriyah.

"The Marine convoys would bunch up at the foot of the bridge, and we would see their troops get ready," explained the UK Battery G's Sgt. Pearce, "and then at 'Go', we'd fire all our 105s, and the Marine howitzers behind us would fire, and the convoys would race up through the city."

"Lieutenant Shea was great when we were firing these missions," Cpl. Czombos said. "He came around to the gun line and told us what we were shooting, and so we knew that we had to be dead perfect. I'd heard about the Marines getting ambushed, so this was our first real chance to fuck up the Iraqis but good."

The batteries would fire a mission, aimed at a location on their dirty grid map known only by the FDCs and recorders like LCpl. Lamb, Phil, and their section chiefs. As their rounds landed, the Marine 7-tons and transports would race north up Highway 7 through Nasiriyah. "It was fucking awesome," LCpl. Bechu remembered later. "They went past us, with their guns outboard, putting out thousands of fucking rounds as they went up the highway; it sounded like a hugest firefight as they went through the city."

By the middle of the afternoon, Charlie Battery had fired four of these missions, along with four Immediate Suppression (IS) missions. In the middle of the day, at 1445, Phil and Lamb, along with Bravo and Alpha batteries, received another IS mission. This mission escalated into some extensive shelling, and when it ended, the three batteries had accounted for the destruction of eleven Iraqi armored personnel carriers and many Iraqi soldiers—and they'd protected numerous Marine convoys.

When this latest mission was completed, at approximately 1530, 1/10 thankfully received its first ammunition re-supply. Charlie Battery had crossed the border some 90 hours previously and had been involved in this nonstop battle for the past 35 hours. In the past several hours, Marine Command had ordered them to begin vetting (decreasing) their fire mission orders in order to conserve ammunition. In fact, Charlie Battery was running so short of high explosive (HE) rounds that they began firing rocket-assisted projectile (RAP) rounds in the rocket-off mode, and scaled back the charge to a #3 Green Bag, which is less powerful. Fortunately, with the mid-afternoon re-supply, the battery received approximately 120 HE and 100 DPICM rounds, along with the requisite supply of charges and fuses, and Phil and the others were able to fire as necessary.

Phil and Charlie Battery were only 35 hours into the battle, which proceeded to escalate into the evening and night hours.

With LCpl. Lamb calling out the fire missions to Phil, who related them to his brother Marines on Gun #1, they were in non-stop motion as Battalion CP trained the guns of 1/10, 1/11, and the British Battery G on multiple targets. Simultaneously, the US and British commands integrated the "Arthur Radar" into the American radar net and the 42 combined guns worked together to mass the killing fires of three and four batteries at a time of multiple fire missions. "The engineers bermed us in," Phil said, "and we fired illum (illumination) rounds through the night in order to light the battlefield for the other Marines."

By evening's end, the massed British and American Marine artillery had engaged and destroyed three tanks, two heavy machine gun positions, two "technicals" (pick-up trucks with mounted machine guns in the truck bed), and eleven other vehicles, as well as two Iraqi infantry battalions. In between these missions, they had also fired numerous Code Red missions, which enabled the Marine supply columns to continue racing north to Baghdad.

At one point, the newly combined USA-UK radar detachment detected an Iraqi artillery battery that had again halted 2/8's Infantry advance and had them pinned down in an awkward and exposed position. The massed Marine and British Airborne batteries quickly engaged and destroyed the Iraq artillery, and 2/8 was able to then proceed through the city.

Without rest or let-up, Phil, Jones, Lamb, Noyes, and their Charlie Battery friends, as well as all the other Marine artillery batteries, continued to shoot well past dark, as they received fire missions from their FDCs throughout the night, and thus continued to fire until dawn broke.

1/10 artillery taking it to the Iraqis at night

Their new mates from Battery G kept just as busy during the evening, as the number of fire missions called in seemed to increase. "We got some of the better missions," said Sgt. Pearce, "especially since we had Captain Andy Newsham up with the Marine FDCs getting us the work." A rugby player, Captain Newsham stands 6'6" and is as gung-ho as any Marine. His enthusiasm carried over into both the Marine and UK ranks, and soon his Battery G artillerymen were firing their smallest charge (Charge 1) through the power wires at targets only 1,000–1,200 meters away. "We were firing our HE rounds fused to explode only 9 meters (28 feet) off the ground," said Sgt. Dickinson. "We could see the Iraqis we were shooting!"

Battle Confusion

"I was in the TAC-CP," said Chaps Ritchie. "We were listening to the Marine cross-talk on the radio net, and we couldn't believe how confusing the battle was becoming. We didn't know what was fact or what was opinion. It was a mess. We had no clue about actual casualties, wounded, or even enemy strengths."

Back home, I watched a television clip of two Marines standing behind palm trees shooting at two Iraqi soldiers who were literally 20 yards away, just across the road—so much for the antiseptic, high-tech war promulgated by the Pentagon. "This is like watching a History Channel show on fucking Iwo Jima," I told anyone who asked me how Phil was faring. "How can the Pentagon keep saying that Nasiriyah has been secured?"

With this kind of fighting raging through the city, the 1st MEF Marine troop and supply convoys were simply unable to roll safely through Nasiriyah. "The battle had deteriorated to a confusing mass of small units fighting each other, which was exactly the type of urban warfare we wanted to avoid," Lt. Col. Grabowski said later.

Under Friendly Fire

Charlie Battery was fortunate that the engineers had bermed them in the prior day. Shortly after the first fire mission of the evening, after the sun had set, some trigger-happy and nervous Marines from RCT-1's LAVs began ripping into their ranks. It seemed they were firing at the muzzle flashes from Pvt. Barr's and Phil's howitzers. Despite the fact that Charlie Battery had been in the same position for two days, and these RCT-1 Marines had been watching them fire throughout the day (and their muzzle flashes were

How could they not know who we were? They'd watched us fire all day!

LCpl. Sobola Bechu

all pointed outbound), these trigger-happy Marines sprayed Guns 1 and 2 from a distance of only a few hundred yards.

Phil, Barr, and Bechu remembered this vividly. "We had friendly fire coming in on us," Barr said, "At first we had no idea who was firing at us, so we just hit the deck and stayed down. There were rounds bouncing off of the barrel of my howitzer, and ripping through the sides of Lubin's 7-ton."

No one, either Iraqi or Marine from Charlie Battery, was injured in this sorry display of fire discipline, and later that night, RCT-1 moved out towards Baghdad, taking their artillery battery 1/11 with them.

Unfortunately for the Marines of 1/10, the UK's G Battery of the Airborne Brigade was ordered to rejoin their main unit back in the Rumaila Oil Fields at first light. They had fired virtually non-stop through the night, from approximately 2000 to 0330, and had expended some 200+ rounds during the night; and the Marines were sorry to see their UK brothers pull out. As the battle continued through the rising sun of a new day, the Marines were faced with defeating the Iraqis with just the original 18 guns of Charlie, Bravo, and Alpha batteries.

The FOs and infantry observers reported that the artillery had inflicted serious casualties in the Iraqi ranks, as well as caused the loss of a substantial amount of enemy equipment. These efforts enabled the infantry, armor, and AAVs to maneuver and advance as required—yet despite all the firing, the Marines still had not secured the city of Nasiriyah.

Day 5: More Aggressive Fighting

Tuesday, 25 March 2003

Although it was a new day, for Phil and Gun #1's crew, there was no difference now between night and day. The shelling of Nasiriyah continued in both ferocity and anger as Charlie Battery shot numerous fire missions during the dead of night. Command HQ continued calling Red Rain missions, along with engaging counterfire targets as well as targets of opportunity.

Working with that fine balance between hate, anger, and fatigue, Charlie Battery responded to every called mission almost instantly, and at 0330, destroyed an Iraqi infantry battalion that was threatening their infantry.

"I remember hearing our artillery going out the entire time," said Lt. Col. Grabowski. "It was a damn good feeling to know that whatever mission we called back to them to shoot got done, and got done quickly. I didn't know what battery was shooting what mission, but they all were real good that day."

While a typical artillery battery fires at targets miles and miles away, Charlie Battery and 1/10 were almost as actively involved in the battle as was their infantry. That morning, 1st Lt. Shea and SSgt. Fontenoy took the battery advance party to a position within the southern boundaries of the city, where they immediately made contact with some 50 enemy. "They were military age males," said 1st Lt. Shea, "and appeared well-groomed and well-fed. They stood out easily against the poorly clothed, shaggy, and somewhat undernourished locals. Anyway, from around 150 meters off our right flank, they began to surround our position. SSgt. Fontenoy called it first—they were digging in a mortar position. Unfortunately, they had a dozen or so women and children standing directly behind them, which made firing on them problematic at best, and the battalion commander directed us to return. SSgt. Fontenoy and I covered the AP team as it withdrew." Later that evening, the battery was directed to fire a counter-battery on that same position where they saw the Iraqis, thereby proving that the Iraqis were using civilians to mask or shield their maneuvers.

During mid-morning, despite the fatigue of no sleep and the concussion and noise of three days of virtually nonstop shelling, the situation continued to worsen for Charlie Battery as the Iraqis continued to aggressively defend their city. Their 1/2 Infantry was still taking considerable fire from the Iraqi defenders—the same Iraqi defenders Army Intelligence had failed to detect the prior Sunday—so Charlie Battery and their TAC-CP were ordered to move forward into the outskirts of the city and help drive them out.

Despite what the Pentagon was claiming about "desultory Iraqi opposition," the Iraqi Army and civilian irregulars rose to the occasion and drove Charlie Battery out of their new location before they could get bermed-in again. Their situation deteriorated rapidly, so before they were overrun, Main Command and TAC-CP wisely decided to pull back to their initial positions, where they could resite their guns behind the existing berms.

Once they were sited back on the original gun line, Charlie Battery resumed their shelling, as RCT-2 Command needed every round in order to support their 1/2 and 2/8 Infantry still battling in and around the city. "We were short of rounds the entire time,"

Cpl. Hebert said later. "We would let Top and Gunny know about our ammunition status, and we were as worried as they were."

Whether it was an issue of the weather, or that the ferocity of the battle took 1st MEF by surprise, ammunition supply was an issue thru the entire battle.[8] As the Combat Service and Supply Battalion could only deliver what they had on hand, the logistics train had to work very hard to deliver sufficient munitions to the three batteries. "I walked the gun line constantly," said Top Santivasci. "I checked on our ammo status, on how our guns were sited, and just to see how everybody was holding up. Even though I knew Gunny Lambert had done a great job training Charlie Battery, and they were all doing fine, I wanted to keep tabs on everyone."

I couldn't get out to check on my men often enough.

MSgt. Michael Santivasci

Mother Nature Invades

Back home, the television stations were focusing on the weather. For the past several days, all the stations were talking about how the March winds were picking up, and MSNBC was focusing on a giant wind and sandstorm, and whether or not it would delay the Allied military operations when it reached the war zones in southern Iraq.

When the storm finally reached Kuwait and Iraq, the MSNBC and CNN weather professionals told their American audiences that it was one of the worst storms in recent memory. These desert storms—known throughout the Middle East as "shamals"—were a combination of driving rain, heavily gusting winds, and an accompanying sandstorm. While Charlie Battery had some experience in operating in wind and sandstorms when in Camp Shoup, nothing had prepared them for what they encountered outside of Nasiriyah that day.

At one point, the cameras on MSNBC's "Bloommobile" could barely spot the M1 Abrams tank that was only some 20 meters ahead of it. David Bloom had to shout into his microphone in order to be heard over the howling of the wind and the noise of his M88; and as the winds gusted and swirled, I could barely see the tank he was following. The enthusiasm of the war's opening days "7th Cav.'s Race to Baghdad" suddenly seemed to be disappearing in the face of reality.

The newsmen were reporting that Allied military operations were being halted by the storm. I assumed (and hoped) that Iraqi operations were equally stopped. From the MSNBC report of the past Saturday night, I knew Phil was in Nasiriyah (which the Pentagon kept insisting "had been secured"). During this time, the winds picked up to howling, unimaginable levels, and as a raging sandstorm hit Nasiriyah, almost all Allied operations were halted—except for Charlie Battery.

Phil remembered it all too well. "They sent me out in that nasty sandstorm to set the aiming posts. Even with my goggles, I couldn't see for five yards, and at the same time, we were taking incoming fire. I had to go out in the desert by myself and set the stakes at 50 and 100 meters. If I set them wrong, then all our aiming would be wrong. Of course, I set them correctly, Dad, but that was the most scared I was."

At this point, a dug-in Iraqi T-55 tank ambushed a 2/8 patrol. The tank was dug-in to the east of Highway 7, and was in position to halt every convoy running up Ambush Alley. The raging sand and winds were so fierce that neither A-10 Warthogs or the vaunted Blackhawks could fly in order to support the Marine infantry, and *The New York Times* was reporting that the weather had halted all American military operations.

Marine artillery continued, however, and despite howling winds and blowing sand strong enough to affect the TOWs fired at the tank by 2/8—Charlie Battery rose to the occasion and used their DPICMs to destroy the tank.

Gunny Lambert was right—when under stress and pressure, a Marine's training takes over, and Phil had set the aiming posts correctly. The Charlie Battery guns continued to fire accurately, and so the highway through Nasiriyah remained reasonably clear. With their artillery protection, the Marine convoys continued to roll north to Baghdad.

During the late afternoon, the sandstorm turned into a drenching thunderstorm that turned the entrenched Charlie Battery gun line into a swampy, soupy, and muddy mess. The weather did not halt the Iraqi's ferocious defense of their city, however, and Charlie Battery continued to respond to fire missions as they were received.

The unit was already beat from days of no sleep, moving up to the LoD, and the first days of the battle. Now they had to shoot missions and live in what Phil described as "slop." Lance Corporal Bechu remembers the misery too, especially after he viewed a photograph of himself and his buddy, Cpl. Hebert, following the worst of the rainstorm.

> We couldn't see for shit! We all just did the best we could.
>
> *LCpl. Nicholas Lamb*

> I have never been so miserable in my life. It was a cold, drenching rain, like a November rain in Pennsylvania.
>
> *LCpl. Phil Lubin*

Hebert and Bechu trying to warm up after the rainstorm

"It was wet sand, and we sank in it up to our boots, so we were wet and cold the whole time. We would eat our MREs between our fire missions, or try to brew some coffee in order to take the chill off us."

Day 6: Intense Iraqi Resistance
Wednesday, 26 March 2003

As Phil and Charlie Battery dragged themselves through the mud and mess during the heavy downpour and kept firing, the battle continued to increase in both lethality and intensity. The FOs and TAC-CP continued to identify and initiate both incoming calls for fire (CFF), as well as counter-fire targets. At approximately 1115, Charlie Battery and the other batteries were ordered to fire on a hospital that the FOs confirmed was serving as a Fedayeen strongpoint. Lt. Col. Dunahoe's 3/2 Infantry had been trying unsuccessfully to dislodge the Fedayeen from the building, and so called in a mission for the artillery to dislodge the defenders brutally and effectively. "It was a Battalion 3 mission," Phil said later. "Every gun put three rounds on the same target at the same time." Cpl. Czombos bragged, "We used all our concrete piercing rounds on it, and then as a battery, we dropped DPICM on the place within about five minutes. Oh man, we fucked it up good!"

Even after the rainstorm finally blew itself out, the Iraqis never let up. In contrast to what the news and the government spokesman reported daily about Nasiriyah being secured, not only was the city many days from being secured, but the Iraqis continued their attempts to mount an offensive against the Marines. "We didn't know it at the time," said Lt. Col. Grabowski, "but later we learned that the Fedayeen were being helped by Egyptians, Syrians, and Palestinians. It makes sense now, but during those days, we were just amazed at their continued resistance."

Despite the Marines almost nonstop shelling, the Iraqis appeared again at approximately 1500, which led to the heaviest day of firing yet for Charlie Battery and 1/10's two other batteries. Since the weather had finally cleared, the Marine Command and TAC-CP were now able to receive battlefield information from aerial FOs and 1/10's unmanned drones. With this live-time information, the battalion ordered 15 more fire missions from Charlie Battery. "I spent as much time as I could on the gun line with my Marines," said 1st Lt. Shea. "If I wasn't passing orders or situational updates, I would just stay on the gun line and make sure everyone was OK."

Targets on Day 6 were situated in every corner of the city. They varied from a refueling depot to small groups of mobile Fedayeen, to yet more artillery batteries. Marine Intelligence had been working overtime, as they realized that many of the units and weapons 1/10 had been shelling seemed to belong to many Iraqi units, not just the Iraqi 11th Infantry, who they had learned was defending the city. From both the massive amount of equipment as well as the unexpected types (T-62 tanks, for example), the Marines began to suspect that the Iraqi troops in Nasiriyah were receiving some substantial reinforcements.

As Phil and his Gun #1 crew continued to concentrate on their own special world behind the berm, they learned later they had been an integral part of the destruction of 44 Iraqi artillery pieces, an ammunition dump, five D-30 batteries, two Type-59 Republican Guard batteries, two refueling depots with APCs and trucks, several defended buildings, a military complex, and an Iraqi Infantry convoy that had been speeding into action against 1/10's Infantry; they had inflicted more than 400 Iraqi casualties. And Wednesday was far from finished.

Through the course of the day, TAC-CP had been offered repeated counter-fire targets in the southern sector of the city, in the region of the main Nasiriyah train station. For a variety of reasons, but primarily because of the risk of massive civilian casualties, permission to proceed on the fire missions had been continually denied. As the sun was setting on this ugly day, however, the situation suddenly changed.

While Marine Command had been receiving intelligence from various Iraqi

Jones waits by his gun for a fire mission

sources, they had no FOs on the ground of their own to verify what they'd been told. During the course of the afternoon, however, they began to realize the reports of approximately 1,000 irregular and Fedayeen forces were accurate, especially when added to the repeated reports of hard targets. Suddenly, news came across the Radio Battalion Network that not only were 2,000 irregulars and Fedayeen gathering at the city's railway station, but they were preparing to launch a substantial counterattack. Wasting no time, Marine Command sent Charlie Battery and the other guns an immediate fire mission of ten rounds of Dual Purpose Improved Conventional Munitions (DPICMs), which resulted in enormous Iraqi casualties within the next ten minutes at that railroad station.

A "Battalion 10" Event

A fire mission of ten rounds by the entire battalion is called a "Battalion 10." With the battalion having 18 howitzers, each one firing 10 rounds, this awesome display of artillery fire is why artillery is known as "The King of Battle." Even during the important Code Red missions, where they protected their Marines driving up Ambush Alley, the Marines had spent the previous days firing missions of 2-3-5 rounds each. Suddenly, however, a mission was called down to the gun line that brought the Marines to a fever pitch of excitement.

First Lieutenant Shea related the "Battalion 10" mission, which he felt was one of the highlights of the Battle of Nasiriyah:

> It was evening, and I was sitting on an MRE box in the center of the battery with Gunny Lambert, SSgt. Fontenoy, 1st Sgt. Winstead, as well as Lt. Humble and SSgt. Dominguez, when we heard the mission come over the radio. Without a word, we looked at each other in amazement, and ran down to the gun line to help—after days of firing 2-3 round missions, a Battalion 10 is quite an event, and the boys exploded with excited yelling and clanging. When I wasn't helping to load and ram, I was hitting them on their backs and helmets to motivate them. I was running up and down that gun line like a cheerleader!
>
> I was loving every minute of it! Seeing those Marines fire over three tons of ammunition in as many minutes. As the third and fourth rounds were being loaded into our

It was 'steel rain' and we fucked them up!

Cpl. Jorge Delarosa

guns, we could see the first volley functioning over the target. It was all DPICMs we fired, and it was easy to see from our position.

The Marines of Charlie, Bravo, and Alpha batteries had just dropped 180 rounds of DPICM rounds on the Nasiriyah train yard. Each DPICM was fused to explode in the air over a target and scatter its 88 smaller bomblets that explode once they hit the ground. So 15,840 small bombs quickly blasted the Iraqis who were gathering to attack the Marines.

After the Battalion 10 mission, Phil and his fellow gun crew Marines heard they had killed 3,000 Iraqis, and later, people were saying that "our arty had won the battle." At the time, however, Phil was too tired to care. It was an intense and exhausting fire mission. "I heard that we'd vaporized the rail yard," Cpl. Gault said. "2,000? 3,000? Who cares? We got them all!"

Although it was not initially apparent in the muck of the evening, by stopping the Iraqi counterattack here, Phil and his Charlie Battery mates on their howitzers, along with Bravo and Alpha battery, were later credited by Brigadier General Richard Natonski, 2nd MEF and Task Force Tarawa's commanding general, with "breaking the back of the enemy forces defending Nasiriyah."[9]

Iraqi Counterattack

Despite the Battalion 10 barrage, the Iraqis still refused to quit. As the sun set at approximately 1800, Infantry 2/8's CP came under direct attack. The Iraqi counterattack included the surviving portion of the group hit at the Nasiriyah train station, and their spirited counterattack carried close to the RCT-2 CP. Bravo Battery jumped up on their berm and fought them off with their crew-served weapons.

"I realized things were getting serious," said Phil, "when Gunny and SSgt. Fontenoy came around and issued us grenades and told us to man the berms and be ready to defend ourselves. We're an arty battery, so I knew that this wasn't good."

Yet as the situation behind Charlie Battery's berm became serious, Phil also remembered a situation that involves a rather funny story for him, but not-so-funny for LCpl. Bechu. Phil related how "some of the guys had taken a dump on the berm, so when Gunny told us to get up there and defend ourselves, I told Bechu where

> When Gunny told us to jump on the berms with our M16s, I began thinking that maybe things weren't going so well.
>
> *LCpl. Phil Lubin*

to lie down, and I got him to lie in a big one!" Bechu just shook his head as Phil recounted the story, and added, "It really didn't bother me then. I just moved over a little; I guess I was concentrating on keeping a lookout for the Iraqis."

Top Santivasci added a much more sobering note, however, to the deteriorating situation, "What the boys didn't know at the time was that when Bravo jumped off their gun to drive off the Iraqis, back in HQ we were getting ready to destroy the radio codes and other classified items. I was up with one of my guns at that point; the Iraqis just weren't quitting."

Bravo Battery was only some 500 meters outside of the city, so they received the brunt of the attack. In their efforts to help drive off the Iraqi troops, Charlie and Alpha batteries lowered the barrels of their howitzers to almost horizontal, and they fired point-blank into the advancing Iraqis. "We were shooting No. 2 Green bags," said Phil, "which we were then cutting in half in order to chop down our range. We were shooting at targets like 700 meters away, instead of our normal ten miles away. This was a real fight!"

Afterwards, Gunny Lambert complimented the young Marines on how they handled themselves. It was a very exciting and anxious time as the unit was taking some small arms fire. Gunny was emphatic that people know "The boys did great; and they should be proud of the job they did."

Once again, 2/8 urgently requested fire support from 1/10, but at the same time, C Company 2nd LARs arrived on the scene, which unfortunately, served to confuse the fire mission as C Company was too close to the Iraqis, and HQ was reluctant to order a fire mission that could well result in Marine fatalities. LCpl. Lamb, therefore, received orders from CP for three Immediate Suppression missions, along with firing continuous illumination rounds, and Phil, Bechu, Hebert, and the others came off the berm to man their howitzers as Charlie Battery's 155mm rounds again kept 2/8 from being overrun.

No one at home knew about any of this, but perhaps we sensed what our sons and husbands were experiencing, and dealt with it as best we could. Lisa Santivasci remembers Nasiriyah through the eyes of her son, Raymond, whose tenth birthday was 26 March 2003. "Our family tradition is we get a piñata for the birthday boy. Well, this year we decorated it as Saddam Hussein. The kids beat it to pieces, and then took it outside and beat the pieces. They loved it! They seemed to have their own 'kid support system', since most of their dads were away fighting, they all felt good or bad together. As a mom, I tried to keep their rumors and questions in check, because I knew they were comparing my answers with their friends, and vice-versa."

Leah Starner, Cpl. Hebert's fiancé, talked of how she also hated those days during the Battle of Nasiriyah. "It was horrible. I told myself not to watch TV, but then I drove myself crazy by not knowing. So I looked in the papers for casualty figures and names, and then just fidgeted the rest of the day."

For my own part, I went around in a cold, quiet rage. I was unable to help my son when I felt he needed me most, and I just hoped someone took offense to something I did or said, so I could relax in a serious fight.

Day 7: Firebase Pokorney

Following the Iraqi counterattack from the previous evening, Lt. Col. Starnes and 1/10's command decided to consolidate and harden their positions. They used the morning to move the three batteries into a firebase, which was a bermed-in oval approximately one kilometer in diameter, with 42 crew-served weapons and five Avenger anti-aircraft vehicles defending it. Upon completion, the base was christened "Firebase Pokorney" in honor of 1st Lt. Fred Pokorney, 1/10's earlier casualty.

Ignoring the engineers berming-in the area, Charlie Battery handled sporadic fire missions. At the same time, each battery was tasked to conduct security and reconnaissance patrols, and they ensured that the terrain surrounding Firebase Pokorney was secure.

Thursday, 27 March 2003

1st Lt. Fred Pokorney remembered
©Sean Shea

Day 8: The Battle Is Over

Although no one knew it at the time, the battle had reached its climax two days prior on Wednesday, 26 March, when Phil and Charlie Battery shelled and destroyed the Nasiriyah train station, and the 2,000 or more Iraqis readying for their final counterattack. When 1/10 command had been able to spend the prior day building Firebase Pokorney, and this day proved even quieter, both the Marine Command and the Marines on the gun line began to realize that the Battle of Nasiriyah was effectively over—and that it had been won by the unrelenting and accurate shelling of the 1/10 artillery batteries.

Friday, 28 March 2003

Well, unfortunately for you, Sir, that 13% is U.S. Marines!

Colin Powell, in reply to an Iraqi reporter who claimed only 13% of Americans knew where Iraq was located

At last, the Charlie Battery Marines got a chance to catch up on sleep, on eating, and just sitting in the mud and muck left over from the rainstorm, the sandstorm, and then the battle. Little things began to mean a lot. As Cpl. Czombos remembered, "What was great was that Lt. Shea would come around in the evenings and try to keep us filled in on what was going on in the war around us. I appreciated his efforts and attention. He's one good XO."

Days 9–12: Looking Back on a Job Well Done

Saturday, 29 March to Tuesday, 1 April 2003

With the battle seemingly finished, 1/10's command began to tally up the statistics. They had to do them more than once, as they were astonished at what the raw numbers showed—what their three artillery batteries had accomplished was simply stunning. In the seven days from the start of the battle until the Wednesday they took out the train station, our young Marines of Charlie Battery, along with their battery-mates in Bravo and Alpha, had accepted and completed some 200 fire missions, and shot some 2,140 rounds! Had they not suffered from a chronic shortage of ammunition through the entire battle (the Pentagon protests to the contrary), they could have fired several hundred rounds more per gun during the same time period.

Yet neither the battle nor the war was finished.

Although command and the batteries did not realize it until much later, their shelling and subsequent destruction of the Nasiriyah train station (along with killing or wounding the 2,000 Iraqi troops), caused the enemy to realize they could not win against the Marines. The amount of daily fire missions declined drastically, as the FOs and infantry found fewer and fewer worthwhile targets.

A Revealing Interview with an Iraqi Commander

That's why the Battle of Nasiriyah was such a slugfest; they thought they'd do the same damn thing to us as they did to the 507th.

Lt. Col. Rick Grabowski

Only afterwards did the stunning truth get revealed on how this eight-day battle unfolded. The truth of the matter was brought to light when Lt. Col. Grabowski completed an interrogation with the executive officer of the Iraqi 23rd Infantry Brigade, who had been captured by Bravo Company 1/2.

Grabowski related the details of the debriefing with this Iraqi commander, who told him thru a Kuwaiti interpreter, how surprised the Iraqis had been when the Americans had fled from his soldiers instead of fighting. Because of this weak showing, the Iraqi soldiers began to reform in the city in order to fight.

Initially, Grabowski didn't quite understand these comments from his Iraqi counterpart. On the contrary, he recalled the Marines coming in "harder and faster than necessary." It was only later that Grabowski realized the officer was referring to the Army's 507th maintenance company who had stumbled into Nasiriyah in a failed attempt to catch up with their main Army company. The Iraqi commander—along with his soldiers—had confused the 507th maintenance unit with his Marines. Immediately, Grabowski realized the whole Battle at Nasiriyah had been due to the Iraqis confusing the Army's inability to fight with the Marine's inability to quit.

Basically, Grabowski gathered from this debriefing that some 60% of Iraqi troops had deserted, but when the 507th had fought so poorly, the regular army units came back to fight the Marines. "Suddenly, they were not intimidated by Americans at all. What was worse was that it motivated the Fedayeen to fight, and they were a thorn in our side the entire time."

News of the interrogation and what it revealed ran quickly through the officers, senior NCOs and enlisted men of RCT-2, and the common feeling was "the whole battle was a big mistake; it was all because of the 507th didn't know how to fight."

Despite this initial wrong impression by the Iraqis, Grabowski couldn't help but admit and wonder, "The Iraqis had fought very hard, and frankly, very fiercely, and we were very concerned by this. If it was so bad here, how bad would the fighting be when we got to Baghdad?"

> **After we saw you take those heavy casualties on the first day and you continued to attack, my men cut and ran.**
>
> *A captured Iraqi officer*

Securing Nasiriyah

On Saturday, RCT-2 welcomed the 15th MEU into Nasiriyah, who was tasked with clearing another sector of the city, along with relieving RCT-2's forces. In the last two days, Phil and Charlie Battery had only received three counter-fire missions, along with five adjust-fire missions, as they supported their 2/8 Infantry clearing the city. This lack of missions indicated that the Marine infantry had finally succeeded in securing most of the city, and the Battle for Nasiriyah was coming to an end.

But then on the 30th, a C-130 gunship cruised slowly over the city, pouring down its amazing volume of fire for most of the night. "It was just awesome," Phil told me later. "The plane just flew in circles, firing its gatling gun, a Bofors gun, and even a 105mm howitzer. It was like an all-night fireworks show!"

The next day was also a slow day. "We got our hair cut," said Warren, and Noyes recounted how they had to actually police the area and begin to pick up trash. "Hey, we won!" he said. "Let the Iraqis keep the place clean!"

War Stories from Home

Back home, all I knew was that every day for the last several days, Pentagon spokesman, Torrie Clark, kept announcing that Nasiriyah, like Basra, was "secured." If the city was so secured, then why are they still fighting? And why are they announcing it every day? While I liked the ideas of the embedded reporters, these announcements seemed to fall into the category of "not enough news"; I knew Phil was in Nasiriyah, but no one really seemed to understand what the situation was.

Not to mention, the peace rallies and the anti-war demonstrations were reaching a fever pitch that weekend. While I dismissed the demonstrations from around the world as the whining of uninformed Euro-faggots, I was distressed at the reactions shown from our own American cities. In all the bigger American cities, it seemed that most of the TV news was comprised of interviews with anti-war protesters.

A distressing number of them were of my own age group, as well as others who should have remembered how divisive these types of comments were during the Vietnam War years. The chip on my shoulder had grown much larger during the week Phil was fighting in Nasiriyah, and I decided it was best if I stayed out of public places like shopping malls. There was an excellent possibility of my starting a serious brawl if I happened onto some sort of peace demonstration, so I did my best to simply stay away.

As it turned out, other parents and friends had the same problems. Lucille Warren recalled getting into an argument at work over the war and telling one of her co-workers, "I don't want to hear about your politics!" Likewise, Leah Starner also defended her fiancé, Cpl. Hebert, at her workplace. One of her co-workers who knew Hebert and knew he was fighting in Iraq kept pushing her anti-war opinions on Leah. "I had to tell her to shut the fuck up. It was better for her that she didn't talk to me again."

Fortunately for Leah, the patients in the speech pathology office where she worked more than made up for her co-worker. "All the older patients, the WWII and Korean War vets, would always ask me how Cory was doing, and then tell me how they were former Marines too. They kept me sane through this, and it was beautiful." She also garnered encouragement one day from some former Vietnam-era Marines who were attending a pro-US war demonstration in her town. "I stopped the car and joined them, and just cried. It was such a relief to see these guys, and see how they appreciated what Cory was doing."

My son is over there fighting! You just shut up!

Lucille Warren

In Ohio, out in Middle America, Paul Czombos refused to leave his house except to go to work or for basic shopping. "I was afraid that if I went to a mall and saw some of these people in a peace demonstration, I'd lose my cool and start a fight. My son is out on the line, risking his life for these idiots, and I knew I couldn't afford to end up in a fight over their cowardliness."

Day 13: Jessica Lynch Rescue

Wednesday, 2 April 2003

Early in the night hours of 2 April, a small contingent of Delta Force operators conducted a raid on a Nasiriyah hospital, which was rumored to hold some American POWs, specifically, PFC Jessica Lynch, who was last seen by Charlie Battery and the Marines as she and the 507th careened wildly through the desert some nine days earlier.

Phil and Charlie Battery were given the diversion mission to shoot, and they fired on and destroyed their targets; an arms cache, as well as a suspected Iraqi command post. The Special Operations Force was equally successful and swooped down on the hospital where they rescued PFC Lynch and also returned with the bodies of seven American soldiers who had been buried in the hospital courtyard. Thus, Phil, Gun #1, and Charlie Battery fired the last mission during the Battle of Nasiriyah.

Letter from Phil:

1 April 2003

Hi, Dad,

What's going on there? Well, war is fun. So far our battery has around 2,500 confirmed kills including person-nel, tanks, artillery & civilians. I have got some great sto-ries for you. When I get back, ask me about the army & the west bridges, and enemy mortars. We're the most talked about unit over here. I'm sure you're hearing about the Battle of Nasiriyah. We are set up two miles outside the city & our battalion pretty much took it over. The Army people that were captured were right up the road from us. They found the female today. We've been shelling the town since 0430 this morning.

There is so much I want to tell you, but it's too much to write down, so ask me about the Army convoy, being attacked, the inner city, when I get back. Oh yeah, & a blown up USMC tank.

I pretty much just wanted to write & say I'm doing good, just tired & dirty and we're killing Arabs by the thousands. In addition to the 2,500 confirmed kills, we've supposedly killed a regiment of about 3,000, but the place was completely vaporized.

I miss you and hopefully, I'll be back this year, but we're hearing rumors of a 13-month tour, but who knows?

Talk to you later.

Their Place in Marine History

After the Jessica Lynch mission, the day dawned as one for the men of Charlie Battery to just relax. No more fire missions. No nothing. They just slept, ate, and rested. The most stressful activity was getting cleaned up for their battery and platoon photos, and later in the day, they loaded their gear for their next day's travel to Ad-Diwaniyah.

Such a relaxing day belied the previous week, when these young men and their fellow Marines in Charlie Battery made a name for themselves fighting the fiercest, most intense battle of Operation Iraqi Freedom. The Battle of Nasiriyah will be remembered as the battle that taught the Iraqis the Marines could not be defeated, and that further mano y mano resistance was futile.

This was quite an initiation for a group of Marines who, with the exception of 1st Lt. Shea and Gunny Lambert, had never seen combat before they crossed the LoD only nine days previously. Existing on cold MREs and sleeping in the mud next to their gun for an hour or two (when they could), these young men showed the Iraqis, the world, 1st Lt. Shea, Gunny, and, more importantly, themselves exactly the amount of balls, courage, and tenacity it takes to be a combat Marine.

Months afterwards, Pvt. Barr had a proud perspective on the battle, along with his role, and that of his friends. "I tried to look out for the other guys ... I could look over and see Lubin kicking ass on Gun #1; he was into it. Jones was kicking ass on my gun. And I knew Gunny and Top and the others were watching over us because you look out for your friends in this kind of shit. Now I understand the monuments and stories I saw at Belleau Wood, and all the Marine Corps history we learned in boot camp."

Now you can add the Marines of Charlie, Bravo, and Alpha batteries from 1st Battalion, Tenth Marines (and their 18 howitzers) to those stories of Marine tradition that stretch from Belleau Wood to Tarawa and to the dirty outskirts of An Nasiriyah.

Standing left to right are: 1st Lt. Sean Shea, the Guns Platoon Commander; SSgt. S. L. P. Bolton, the Section Chief for howitzer #6; SSgt. M. E. Dominguez, Motor T Chief; SSgt. A. M. Green, Communications Chief; 1st Lt. M. F. McDonald, Fire Direction Officer and HQ Platoon Commander; SSgt. J. C. Twiggs, Section Chief for howitzer #1; SSgt. P. C. Brooker, Operations Chief and HQ Platoon Sergeant; and SSgt. J. D. Fontenoy, Guns Platoon Sergeant and Local Security Chief.

Kneeling in front are: 1st Sgt. M. T. Winstead, Battery First Sergeant; Capt. M. A. Woodhead, Commanding Officer; 1st Lt. J. C. Humble, Executive Officer (until April 24); and GySgt. C. G. Lambert, Battery Gunnery Sergeant ©Sean Shea

Chapter 7

Peacekeepers

Small wars demand the highest type of
leadership directed by intelligence,
resourcefulness, and ingenuity ...
... tolerance, sympathy and kindness
should be the keynote of our
relationship with the mass
of the population.

U.S. Marine Corps Small Wars Manual[10]

3 April–10 May 2003

By now, the war was on its last legs, although no one knew it at the time. The 1st MEF and various Army units had troops surrounding Baghdad, Mosul, Kirkuk, and the other cities; our British allies had secured and taken Basra, and the newspapers and televisions were filled with maps and details of the fight to take Baghdad. In the cities and towns leading up to Baghdad, the Iraqis were deserting before the Marines or the Army arrived, and there was less and less fighting taking place as April unfolded.

Therefore, RCT-2 Command ordered Charlie Battery and 1/10 to move out of Firebase Pokorney, and secure and guard the Western Bridge over the Euphrates River. This was an important mission because the 1st MEF was using this route on Highway 1, Main Supply Route Tampa (MSR Tampa), for their convoys running to Baghdad. Commanded by the Battalion XO, Major Phillip Boggs, his three batteries were switched to provisional rifle units in order to guard the bridge. While only Bravo Battery moved their guns, soon all the Marines moved, and living under the bridge, Major Bogg's task force was christened "Task Force Troll."

Charlie Battery and Task Force Tarawa, however, remained in the southern half of the country. Initially, they had two tasks to perform: Their first was to root out any lingering Republican

131

Guard or Fedayeen forces that might still want to fight; and the second, and probably most important, was to keep the supply routes out of Nasiriyah (Highways 1 and 7), open through to Route 27 so the convoys could still roll north to Baghdad with supplies.

On 3 April, Task Force Tarawa began "Follow and Support Missions" throughout southern Iraq. RCT-2 split off their various battalions as each was tasked for selected missions in different parts of the country. In the next days, the different battalions surrounded the 10th Brigade of the Al Nida Republican Guard, helped liberate the city of Diwaniyah, and finally secured Highways 1 and 7 through their entire length.

At this point in time, RCT-2 and Charlie Battery were a group of Marines driving through Iraq in search of a fight. Odd as their mission seemed, 1st Lt. Shea phrased it accurately, "We would basically drive up into a town and ask them if they wanted to surrender or fight, and we were ready either way. What we couldn't figure out was if it was funny or pathetic."

Running Low on Cigarettes & MREs

Charlie Battery packed and secured their guns for a road march, and they began their tour of southern Iraq. With both their M16s and disposable cameras at the ready, Phil and his squad rolled out of Firebase Pokorney in the morning, and arrived in Diwaniyah 200 kilometers (120 miles) and eight hours later. They established

Diwaniyah
Thursday, 3 April 2003

their gun positions south and east of the city, and then dug in for the night. It was a quiet night; there were no problems or fighting.

In the aftermath of the fighting and worry of Nasiriyah, Phil and his friends began to return to normalcy, and took on more pressing worries such as boredom and an acute lack of cigarettes. Phil recounted, "We drove at like 20 mph in the dust all day. It took all freaking day just to go to another stupid Iraqi town."

Supply shipments had been interrupted during the Battle of Nasiriyah, as ammunition shipments had taken

Bechu and Phil on the road march

After eating MREs every day for six weeks they weren't my favorite food. But when I found out I could only have one per day, that really sucked!

LCpl. Philip Lubin

Ash Shumali
Friday, 4 & 5 April 2003

precedence. Initially, Charlie Battery and the other units of Task Force Tarawa were reduced to eating only one MRE per day. The one-per-day rationing continued after the battle because Army logistics were not up to the task of supplying the required material.

Even worse, the extra cigarettes the Marines had bought on *Ashland* had long been smoked, and the cigarette shortage reached crisis levels. Never short on imagination, the Marines began to take matters into their own hands and they either bought cigarettes from the locals or traded MREs. "The local cigarettes tasted and smelled like dried shit," said Cpl. Czombos, "and the Iraqi kids were trying to hump them to us at two to three dollars each, the little bastards!" But it was Cpl. Gault who admitted they'd hit rock-bottom, when he told me, "We had to buy their cigarettes, shitty as they were, because we'd run out, and were actually breaking open the teabags in our MREs, and were trying to smoke the tea."

Impressions of the Locals

The road show continued, and they left Diwaniyah in the morning. While the day's drive was far shorter than the day before, the weather was changing rapidly from the cold and drizzle and the winter windstorms of Camp Shoup to oppressive heat and dust with temperatures reaching the mid-high 90s. Phil, LCpl. Warren, LCpl. Turcotte, and the others sweated and cursed in the back of their Humvees and 7-tons, and when they finally arrived in Ash Shumali, they secured their perimeter, and dug in for the night.

By this time, the many spares that Phil and Charlie Battery had packed back in Camp Lejeune had long since been utilized. RCT-2 was in dire need of a new supply of tires, gun parts, truck batteries, and the like, and the Battalion was expecting to be re-supplied in Ash Shumali. The gear arrived, and Gunny Lambert ensured that proper maintenance was performed, so the guns and trucks were brought back up to fighting standards.

The following day, 5 April, passed equally uneventfully until the evening, when they received orders to fire an Illumination mission. The mission ended quickly. Since no Iraqi forces were actually spotted, LCpl. Lamb received orders to cease-fire and relayed them to Phil, who passed them to the gun crew. The firing ceased as quickly as it had began.

Driving through the little towns and villages is what made the whole experience worthwhile for Cpl. Hebert who was moved when the women and children would come out of their homes cheering and yelling, "USA!" to the passing trucks. "It made me so proud of what I'd accomplished. That's what I signed up to do—we liberated a country and gave those kids a real future, and I was part of it." Turcotte agreed and recalled how when the children came out to greet the approaching convoys, they seemed happy to see them. "I would throw them candy or whatever I could find." Lance Corporal Bechu reflected on how the children had nothing to do with the war, and he felt sorry for them as they drove through the towns and villages.

> I loved driving thru the towns and seeing the women and children come out and cheer 'USA! USA!'
>
> *Cpl. Cory Hebert*

Not all the Marines thought of themselves as conquering heroes, however. Phil was not at all impressed with the local population when they drove through the towns. He remembers the chaos the most. How the children would run out into the streets and scream at them, begging for food and water. In return, many of the Marines would throw their MREs to them, while at the same time trying to keep them clear of the moving trucks. "It was nuts!"

Having served in both Desert Storm in 1991, as well as Somalia in 1993, Top Santivasci had a more mature outlook on the locals. He noticed how the children seemed to respect the American troops, and would willingly tell them what they wanted to know. On the other hand, he had a poor impression of the adults, who lied to them on just about anything, including food, weapons and Iraqi troops. For example, "An Iraqi man would tell us there were no weapons in the village, yet five minutes later, the kids would be trading weapons with us for MREs. It wasn't an attitude that earned the Iraqi men much respect."

Final Fire Mission

This city was the closest Charlie Battery ever got to Baghdad. Despite the hopes of many in the unit, who wanted to go where the action was, they were relegated to the role of peacekeepers. It was a bitter pill to swallow after all their hard work in Nasiriyah. "I was ready to take another shot at them," said Cpl. Gault, "We kicked their asses once. We could do it again."

Numiniyah
Sunday, 6 April 2003

However, the war was running out of steam, although no one knew it at the time. In the morning, Alpha Battery was split off from the main force, as they were ordered back to Diwaniyah in order to provide support for Infantry 2/8, who was securing the town. Later in the afternoon, Bravo Battery received orders to fire what proved to be the final fire mission of 1/10 for the war. They received a firing mission ordering them to fire HE/VT at a suspected mortar position. The suspected Iraqi position disappeared, and Bravo Battery quickly ceased their firing.

Although there was no attempt made to keep missions spread equally through the batteries, it was only fitting that Bravo fired the final mission, as their action balanced out Charlie and Alpha batteries opening the war on 22 March by destroying the Iraqi mortar platoon outside of Jalibah Airfield.

An Unexpected Reprieve

**Qul'at Sukkar
Monday, 7 April 2003**

Phil and Charlie Battery began another road march long before the sun rose. The battalion moved out of Numiniyah at 0330 and drove the approximately 75 miles southeast to the Qul'at Sukkar. Upon arriving at the city, they were joined by the Marines of the 24th MEU, who had driven up directly from Nasiriyah. The previous weeks' battle at An Nasiriyah had changed the dynamics of the war.

Because Britain's Battery G and their Paratroopers had not been needed to secure the airfield, the town had been by-passed by the larger Marine units on their way to Baghdad. The war had not yet directly reached this dusty town of 40,000. As the two Marine units arrived, they must have appeared a fearsome-looking group to the townspeople. With Arabic-language warnings and rock & roll (jury-rigged into the radio net) blaring from their Humvees and their 7-tons towing 155s, the Marines encountered no resistance—and actually very few civilians—as they sped into the town.

Bobko, Barr, and Czombos on an unexpected reprieve

Charlie Battery and RCT-2 were diverted to the local airbase for the night. The airbase was deserted, and the Marines established their camp, and finally, after almost three weeks of unrelenting physical and mental stress, were able to relax. Command was able to give them the order to change out of their MOPP suits, which they'd worn non-stop since moving out of Camp Shoup on 20 March.

The shedding of the MOPPs helped the Marines cool off somewhat as the weather continued to heat up. No more cold rain and sandstorms of the winter "shamals." The Marines were now enduring daytime temperatures that often topped the 100-degree mark. The evenings didn't bring much relief either with temperatures only dropping to the 70s. "It was easier to just sleep on the desert floor," said LCpl. Warren. "So we'd throw our gear down, and sleep next to the trucks."

Everyone in Charlie Battery appreciated the day to relax. It was a time for them to catch their breath and unwind from all the tension they had been living with for so many weeks. The break was well-timed as a new round of enemy encounters were expected.

Later that night, the Charlie Battery Marines and the battalion loaded up for battle again. Sans MOPP suits, they moved out of their encampment at 0300 to locate and destroy the Iraqi 10th Armored Division. As they resumed their road march and began the 60-mile drive west to Al-Amarah, Phil and the others began to ready themselves mentally for the expected battle.

> We were expecting a big battle against an Iraqi armored unit, so I appreciated the day off to unwind.
>
> *Cpl. Justin Noyes*

Tension & Danger Rise Over Iraqi Armored Division

The 10th Iraqi Armored Division had neither moved nor sent any of their units to help fight the Coalition Forces since the start of the war. Whether their inaction was due to fear or disinterest could not be ascertained from a distance, but their continued existence was construed as a threat to Allied forces, so Task Force Tarawa was ordered to defeat it.

Al-Amarah
Tuesday, 8 April 2003

The attack force crawled slowly along the highway. While maddening to the Marines, who were understandably worried about another Nasiriyah-like battle and wanted to simply get on with it, the Marine brass had chosen a plan that was calculated to give the 10th Armored time to choose between fleeing, surrendering, or fighting.

By about 0900, the battalion arrived at the outskirts of Al-Amarah, and Phil and Charlie Battery sited their gun and prepared for battle. Interestingly, Charlie Battery's road trip was evolving into a military tour of the Fertile Crescent. Having fought on the Euphrates River, Charlie Battery was now only six miles from the Tigris, and only 50 miles from the Iranian border. But before they could ponder any of the biblical or archeological significance, they had to defeat the Iraqi unit arrayed against them.

In theory, the Iraqi division was heavily armed. Intelligence claimed that they had 260 armored personnel carriers (APCs), 60+ artillery pieces, 220 tanks, and some 5,000 soldiers. However, the 10th Armored Division had been bombed repeatedly by both

American and British airplanes, and so Marine Intelligence estimated that the Iraqis might now be at only 25–50% of their theoretical strength.

Reducing Iraqi strength was the Marine goal. By overwhelming the Iraqis with air power, the Marines hoped they would surrender instead of becoming involved in another Nasiriyah-like battle with subsequent loss of Marine lives. "The hope was that these forces would not move and would be capitulating," said 1/10 Commander Lt. Col. Glenn Starnes. "But they've showed no sign of capitulating, so they've been hammered with air strikes."[11]

Allied air was instructed to halt their bombing for 48 hours as the Marine commanders negotiated with their Iraqi counterparts. Lieutenant Colonel Starnes' deadline was that morning, and he made good on his word as Charlie Battery and RCT-2 set up their gun line outside of the town. Phil and his friends in Charlie Battery cleaned their 155s, and began to get themselves mentally ready for another battle. "I really didn't want to fight again," said Phil. "I didn't know whether or not we'd all been lucky coming through Nasiriyah, but we were hearing that we were going to go up against an armored group, and I didn't think these guys would be any easier."

After no responses to the Marine Corps' repeated calls for surrender, the Marines brought the issue to the Iraqis. Phil, Hebert, Bechu and the others on Gun #1, Barr and Gallagher on Gun #2, Jones & Gault on Gun #3, and Delarosa and Czombos on Gun #5 all checked and cleaned their howitzers again, as their supporting armor and LAVs spread out around the town. Above them, the Cobra helicopter gun ships fanned out to search for the enemy.

They had to look hard; the enemy had literally run away. Later, the Marines walked into the city without a shot being fired in anger. Lieutenant Colonel Starnes said, "The locals are saying that they stacked their weapons, parked their vehicles, and walked away. Right now there is no enemy that we know of."[12]

If they wanted to surrender, or go hide in the desert, not killing them was OK with me.

LCpl. Carl Warren

Return to Qul'at Sukkar

Qul'at Sukkar
Wednesday, 9 April 2003

At midmorning, the battalion broke camp and returned to their prior camp at Qul'at Sukkar Airfield. Many in Charlie Battery gathered around 1st Lt. Shea's radio and listened to the BBC announce that Baghdad had been captured by the joint Marine and Army forces that very morning. [The next day, the Royal Marines secured the city of Basra.] For the first time since they left

Camp Shoup, the entire battalion was able to begin refitting and repairing their vehicles under a normal, semi-relaxed attitude.

Except that no one knew if the war was really over, or if the Fedayeen were waiting for the Marines to relax their guard. "We need to tell the commanders to get with their Marines," Lt. Col. Starnes told his officers, "and tell them the war's not over yet."[13] He wanted his Marines to remain as alert as when they rolled out of Camp Shoup on 20 March. "We're still at war," he stated. When talking with *The New York Times* embedded reporter, Michael Wilson, Starnes added, "... that's how somebody gets hurt."[14]

But nothing happened at Qul'at Sukkar.

So the Marines relaxed in the shade of their APCs and 7-tons and watched their Motor T and maintenance techs attempt to keep the trucks that would take them back to Kuwait in working order.

Return to Numiniyah

After RCT-2 moved out of Qul'at Sukkar, they drove for several hours until they returned to Numiniyah. As they drove through southern Iraq, they saw a lot of wreckage, including destroyed tanks and trucks, mostly from Desert Storm, on the sides of the roads.

11–14 April 2003

When they arrived at Numiniyah, they established a two-battery firebase to the west of the city. Phil and Charlie Battery, along with Bravo Battery, sited their guns and were then transformed into provisional rifle platoons. "We were either supposed to be infantry, or maybe get involved in pacification," said LCpl. Turcotte. "Either way, we didn't do anything, which was OK with me."

Another burnt out Iraqi truck

"No Better Friend, No Worse Enemy"

One Iraqi town blended into another by this time. The daily temperatures regularly touched 100 degrees with nightly lows in the 70s. Everyone was dirty. Marine water supplies were sufficient only for drinking, so the troops remained covered with the sand and fine dust that blew everywhere. "What I remember about Al Kut," said LCpl. Warren, "was how the whole battery seemed to get sick

Al Kut
14–22 April 2003

at the same time. I got the squirts first, and within about two days, we all had the runs. I guess it was dirt, fatigue, bad water, who knows? But we all had a miserable couple of days."

During this time period at Al Kut, Chaps Ritchie made the most of the postwar "Stabilization Operation" period by making four trips to Babylon. Eventually, he took a total of about 150 Marines with him, and they toured the city. "What an opportunity this was! This is where the Old Testament located the Leaning Tower of Babel, and here we are, the first Westerners in maybe 30 years traipsing through the town!" While on these trips, he talked to his Marines about the military and economic reasons for this war, and then related it back to the geopolitics of then and now.

One day, he had the opportunity to speak with a museum curator in the city, who explained how the museum had been looted by the locals during the confusion of the war. These locals were very busy trying to sell these stolen treasures to the troops. As a result of his conversation with the museum curator, Chaps Ritchie talked to the Marines and tried to explain why they shouldn't be buying these souvenirs, and then they passed a helmet around and raised money for the museum.

> To be a minister, and be with the Marines in Babylon—this is something I will never forget!
>
> Gordon "Chaps" Ritchie

First Mail in Iraq

The Charlie Battery Marines received mail and packages from home for the first time since they left Camp Shoup back on 19 March. Since their first mail call was on 7 March, and they'd left for the LoD only nine days later, this was the first substantial mail delivery since they'd left Morehead City back in January. "It was great!" said Cpl. Czombos. "I got a bunch of mail and stuff from my dad. And finally we had a lot more magazines to read; we'd been carrying stuff since we got off the ship back in February, and everything we had was falling apart." Like Czombos and the others who received packages and mail, Phil was ecstatic with the small things he'd received from home. Suddenly, he had candy, gum, more cameras, and all sort of lotions and personal items. "We were still pretty dirty, but at least we could clean up a little bit. It was great just to eat something different than MREs for a change."

Some of the items I'd sent Phil were cigars, and I was thrilled to later learn they inspired a photograph that has come to represent his gun crew's self-proclaimed "victory picture." Posing with the cigars I'd sent—despite the fact they were dry from being over two months old—Phil and his fellow Charlie Battery Gun #1 crew lined up for a photograph in front of their gun.

While Phil and crew smoked their cigars to celebrate their first combat, the war was not quite finished. Even though there was no Iraqi government left with whom the Marines or the Coalition could negotiate a surrender, the Marines were left to maintain peace in any way they found appropriate.

Victory cigars

Conflicting Emotions on Peacekeeping Role

The 1st Marine Division has a motto, "No better friend, no worse enemy." In this sort of fluid and variable situation, Charlie Battery and the other Marines of 1/10 and RCT-2 were tasked to keep the peace and maintain civil order, while at the same time remain on alert to be able to move quickly and relentlessly to quell any local unrest or rebellion.

In the Marine's classic book on guerrilla warfare, *Small Wars Manual*, it notes that "in small wars, tolerance, sympathy, and kindness should be the keynote of our relationships with the mass of the population."[15] This book, written in Marine blood during the Banana Wars of the 1920s and 1930s in Central America, forms the backbone of the Marine Corps' ideas of relationships with the local civilian populace. First Lieutenant Shea, Top Santivasci, and Gunny Lambert had studied the book and used it for their guide in instructing Charlie Battery in their dealings with the Iraqi civilians.

As the Charlie Battery and the Marines of RCT-2 began to maintain control of the bridges and roads in southern Iraq, they had to demonstrate to the Iraqi population that Saddam's regime had been removed, and they were the new boss in town. But at the same time, the Marines needed to avoid humiliating the local populace by demonstrating excessive force or performing unneces-

We kicked some ass together, and now we had the picture to remember what we'd done

LCpl. Carl Warren

Victorious Charlie Battery Marines

LCpls Kranz, Souza, and Barr in front of an Iraqi bunker

sary body searches on the women and children.

It is the small things that can help or hinder such a fragile relationship between the local population and foreign troops. For example, Major General James Mattis, commanding officer of the 1st MEF, ordered that the Marines were not to wear sunglasses when patrolling, and to do their best to have normal interactions with the population; something as small and seemingly insignificant as eye-contact and civility was important. He wanted the Marines to be seen as human beings and individuals, not as faceless, armored troops similar to those in a science-fiction movie.

Being both a Marine and the father of two young boys, Top Santivasci looked at the Iraqi civilians with a mixed view. "We might have had only one MRE per day, but we'd put the candy aside and give it to the kids. On the other hand, I didn't trust the adults, and I warned my Marines to keep on their guard."

Some of their Marines, however, managed to put a new angle on American-Iraqi relations, as they actually did pay attention to those many classes back on *Ashland*. Lance Corporal Warren laughed when he related how much he and Charlie Battery had learned about Arab culture and religion. "Since we'd learned a little about the Muslim religion in those cultural classes we took coming over, we separated out all the pork MREs and made sure we gave them to the locals. We didn't have to shoot them; instead, we defiled them!"

Top Santivasci understood that his Marines needed to draw a fine line between war and peace in this confused country. Because no one had officially surrendered and the Iraqi Army simply drifted away, it was difficult to tell if the war was over or not. "We'd see adult men who were probably soldiers, but how could we prove it? And what could we do? Just shoot them? They were unarmed, so we'd just let them go."

Many of the Marines felt sympathy for the women and children, yet had no respect for the men. Corporal Delarosa remembered how they would give MREs to the women and children, and the men would then try to steal them. "The Iraqi men were just shiftless," Cpl. Gault observed. "They were a bunch of pussies. They fought like shit, and then to steal food from their kids? That's pretty pathetic."

Phil hated the peacekeeping operations. In his view, the war was far from over. He had written, "I hate Arabs" on his helmet and tried to intimidate their Iraqi translator, who eventually disappeared. Phil said he never really knew if he could trust him to tell them the truth. "They were all liars and thieves, and they'd just beg for food." The section chief got onto Phil because he kept "racking rounds" (putting a bullet in the chamber of his M16) to protect himself and others. In Nasiriyah, they'd heard about Iraqis pretending to be civilians to get close enough to shoot Marines. Ten Marines were dead from this strategy. Phil recalled, "I'd yell at our guys not to give them food and water; and finally, I convinced Bechu not to be nice to them. I mean, we were still at war."

Lance Corporal Bechu, who was from Zaire and had witnessed civil war and famine firsthand, tended to disagree with Phil on his view. Because of his own personal experience, he viewed the Iraqis from a different perspective. "Yes, we were at war, but it wasn't the fault of the women and children. Lubin was right, but it was still hard not to feel sorry for them."

Phil summed up his argument by saying, "We were still armed and alert at the checkpoints, and I wasn't going to get shot by some stupid Iraqi after everything I'd been through."

Indeed, this was no time for the Marines to relax their guard. An active and aggressive opposition still survived, as the Marine and Army troops in Baghdad were discovering. No one yet knew how to distinguish between friend and foe (and they still don't!). Top Santivasci commented on the difficulties the Marines were having in these peacekeeping operations. "It's a balancing act in this type of environment; it's easy to see both sides of the question. But I let my Marines know that the war was not over, that

> No one really surrendered ... Who could really say whether or not the war was over?
>
> *MSgt. Michael Santivasci*

> We'd been ready to shoot these people, and I saw no reason to let down my guard because the major battles had stopped.
>
> *LCpl. Phil Lubin*

these people were not our friends, and that we had to remain alert every minute."

Letter from Phil:

13 April 2003

What's up, Dad?

There's not much going on here right now. I'll tell you more when I get back, but I'll tell you this: our battalion fought at Nasiriyah. My battery shot around 700 rounds (more than anyone) and killed an estimated 10,000. That's coming from the FOs and the grunts, so I'm not making it up. We also shot the mission that saved the female soldier, so we are getting high praise from everyone.

Now we are further north, near Baghdad, and we're going to start doing humanitarian assistance, which I don't want to do. I hate Arabs. When we drive through cities, it's nuts! Hundreds and thousands of people crowd the streets & shout, "No Saddam! Good Mr. Bush!"

There are all sorts of rumors of when we're coming home, but no one really knows. It will probably be early July, maybe before the Fourth. I'm starting to get mail again, but still no packages. I got letters from you, Gran, Grandmother & Granddad, Mom, Michelle, and Alison & Rick. Right now, we sleep a lot, eat, and are making a tattoo gun, so we're all giving tats, which is fun.

Tattoo session

Marine-Made Tattoos

After reading the last part of this letter, it appeared the lack of mail from Phil might not have been entirely the fault of the post office! I'd sent Phil four packages in the preceding two months, all of which included pens, writing paper, cigars, various small foods and candies, and still more disposable cameras. It never occurred to me that instead of using the pens to write letters, he would break them open and use the ink for a homemade tattoo gun. I heard all about this tattoo gun when Phil surprised me with a phone call on 17 April from Al Kut. According to Phil, Gunny Lambert knew how to make a tattoo gun, and they broke open all the pens I'd sent him and used the ink to tattoo themselves. They tattooed "March 23, 2003" on their forearms. The loss of the pens notwithstanding, it was great to hear from him and know he was in good spirits.

"This was the first time we'd had access to telephones since we left Camp Shoup before we rolled," said Phil later. "I stood in line for over an hour so I could call you and Mom."

Easter in the Holy Land

All the Charlie Battery Marines called home over that Easter weekend, and by Easter Sunday, there were some very happy parents and wives back on

Another tattooed Marine and Phil

the home front. Lance Corporal Turcotte phoned his family on Good Friday, and his mother, Nancy Turcotte, said, "He sounded so good and so relaxed. He said he felt fine and had seen a lot of interesting things in the past weeks. I can't describe to you how relieved I was." Paul Czombos felt the same way when his son, Mike, called on Holy Saturday. "It was like a giant weight was lifted off my chest; I think this was the first time I could breathe in two months."

For Chaps Ritchie, Easter in Iraq took on a special meaning because of where he was. Being in the "cradle of civilization" and where much of the Old Testament was written was a surprisingly popular topic with his Marines, and therefore, he and his fellow chaplains conducted many Bible study classes. "These classes should dispel any ideas of Marines being a bunch of uneducated killers. These

Chaplains of RCT-2 on bank of Euphrates; "Chaps" Richie is 2nd from right

Barr, Aguila, and bermed tents under bridge over the Euphrates River

kids took the classes both for the religion and the history involved." On another level, Chaplain Brian Waite, from 3/2, performed a baptism in the Tigris River on that Easter morning. "Imagine finding Christ, and then on top of that, being baptized in the birthplace of civilization!"

On Monday, 21 April, 1st Lt. Shea and SSgt. Fontenoy moved south again to scout out a new home for Charlie Battery. They and the other advance parties of 1/10 were ordered back to Nasiriyah, in order to prepare for "Stabilization Operations."

"Task Force Troll"

Nasiriyah
22 April–4 May 2003

We provided directions to lost convoys (mostly Army) and I guess we kept the Iraqis from blowing it up.

Cpl. Gaspar Aguila

By this point, the war was over. Baghdad had fallen weeks earlier, and even "Baghdad Bob" had long disappeared off the television. *The New York Times* had ceased including their excellent "A Nation at War" section in their daily paper, and Charlie Battery and the other Marines of Task Force Tarawa were switched to infantry duty as they guarded the bridges back in Nasiriyah. Dubbed "Task Force Troll" the men set up camp under the bridge and kept guard.

The road march back to Nasiriyah was easier this time around. The Marines lived in tents under the bridge, and had a reasonably comfortable existence for the first time since they rolled across the LoD some six weeks previously. Hot meals, regular mail service, packages from home, and time to unwind made their days much more bearable. "Someone got a small football in the mail from home," Cpl. Czombos said, "and we threw it around a lot, and just sort of fucked off." Phil remembers how they got to sit in "real" chairs and live in new tents. "We'd lived in the back of our trucks for months, and you can't imagine how dirty everything was by now."

Although no one in Charlie Battery had the time or interest to investigate ancient history on their first foray through southern Iraq, Nasiriyah is located only a few miles from the ancient biblical city of Ur, the birthplace of the biblical patriarch, Abraham. The biblical history of the region was of interest to more than a few Marines.

One way Marines took in some of the biblical history surrounding them was by attending Gunny Lambert's Bible study classes that he held nearly every evening. Corporal Goodson said Lambert "made the Bible come alive with how he explained where we'd been, and what had happened before us." Doc Sanders agreed how interesting he found the classes. "Religiously, it was all low-key. But Gunny really knows his Bible, so every time I was off-duty, I went and listened to him. Since I hoped I'd never have to come back here, I figured I'd just learn and see everything I could."

Charlie Battery Marines in the back of the 7-ton

"Task Force Troll" duty was more low-key than previous assignments and most remember those days as relatively easy. Basically, they ran a checkpoint on the main highway, but usually they'd only pull over the cars with men in them. Specifically, the Marines were looking for weapons and foreign currency. Although they often found a lot of drugs (mostly hashish), only the weapons and money counted. They would sporadically search women or children, despite the fact many of the children would often asked to be searched. Corporal Aguila said, "Kids thought we were just the coolest people in the world, and would often ask to be searched, but usually, we'd just give them some candy."

Phil enjoyed relaxing under the bridge also. Compared to the duty they'd pulled in earlier weeks, "troll" duty wasn't so bad. While there, the unit adopted a pack of wild dogs. Phil related how the dogs were good for dark nights. "When a Marine would approach, they would normally keep quiet, but when an Arab would approach, they would bark like crazy." Lance Corporal Turcotte remembers one big, older dog that would hang around the men. They named him Cujo. He was a large, shaggy dog with terrible cataracts. Turcotte described him as "the smartest of the pack." Unfortunately, the dogs became too friendly and the senior NCOs didn't like the idea of the men having wild dogs as pets, so they made the younger Marines chase them away.

While stationed under the bridge, Charlie Battery received a lot of attention from the locals. In particular, the Iraqi civilians would try to peddle their wares to the Americans. They were selling Iraqi military helmets, Iraqi money, and Republican Guard soft hats. Marines could buy Republican Guard ID cards, along with Arab clothing and souvenirs like *jallabah*s (long, flowing robes) and *keffiyah*s (turban-like head gear). "We all bought some of the stuff," said LCpl. Warren, "and now I wish I'd bought more."

Sadly, the war was far from finished, however, and it took a tragic accident to show these younger Marines that they are at risk whether they are fighting or not, and that it is impossible for them to be sufficiently careful in such an environment.

Tragedy Strikes Close

On 22 April, a group of Marines had been invited by an Army Special Forces group to join them in a training mission on the grounds of an old Iraqi artillery training school. About one dozen Marines joined them in taking a class on firing a captured Iraqi rocket propelled grenade (RPG). The first two rounds fired successfully, but the third round exploded in the tube, killing three Marines and injuring six more. Chief Warrant Officer (CWO) Andrew Arnold, CWO Robert Channell, Jr., along with LCpl. Alan Lam all died as a result of the accident. The chief warrant officers were the second and third 1/10 casualties of the war.

When the accident occurred, Phil was a couple of hundred yards away, but he didn't see the explosion or accident itself. He and many others heard an explosion, and then suddenly, he said all hell broke loose in the camp. A couple of Humvees went speeding off, and then a few minutes later, some of the first aid choppers came screaming in to pick up the injured Marines. It didn't take long for the news to travel through the troops.

Top Santivasci knew all of the Marines who were involved in the accident, and in fact, had been invited to join them. He'd had to decline the invitation because he was helping to organize a hot meal for the men (the first hot meal in quite some time). "CWO Channell was a great friend of mine. I met him in August, when he joined the battalion, and he and I hit it off immediately." Santivasci was about two klicks (kilometers) away, getting ready to serve that hot meal, when a Humvee came tearing up, and the Marine in the ring mount was shouting, "We have Marines hurt!"

He left immediately with a corpsman and raced to the scene of the accident to see what he could do.

They had already started first aid by the time Santivasci got there, and someone had already called for a Medi-Vac. Lance Corporal Lam had died instantly, but CWO Channell and CWO Arnold were still alive. Even though the Medi-Vac arrived within ten minutes, it seemed like an eternity for those waiting on the ground.

Arnold and Channell aboard USS *Gunston Hall* headed to Iraq

Santivasci jumped in the helicopter with CWO Channell and the doctors for the trip back to the hospital. "Bob was from Alabama, so I kidded him about how bad Alabama football was. I was saying just about anything to keep him conscious. I think he heard me, but he couldn't respond. He'd been up on the berm watching the other men shoot and taken shrapnel in the head, up under the helmet."

LCpl. Lam was already dead, but Andy and Bob were still alive.

MSgt. Michael Santivasci

When they arrived at the hospital, the doctors made him stay outside, but he could still see them working on both men. After about 30 minutes, he saw that CWO Arnold had died, and soon after, a chaplain came out and told Santivasci his friend had passed away as well. "Losing Bob like that, in a training accident, when he'd been through so much dangerous fighting was really hard. I still think of him and the other boys."

Back home, this tragic story on the television news made the war even more personal than ever before for Lisa Santivasci, a Key Volunteer, who had met those young Marines and knew their wives. It made their deaths particularly difficult knowing they had survived the actual war, but they still had perished because of ongoing training operations. It made all the families realize that their men were still in harm's way, and many would not relax until they saw their loved ones back home.

Stabilization Operations

The Stabilization Operations began on 25 April, and each battery received a different task.

Alpha Battery established a permanent traffic control point, along with a battalion "rapid reaction force."

Bravo Battery took control of a petroleum distribution facility and set up a random vehicle checkpoint.

Our Charlie Battery Marines took control of the West Bridge, and established a permanent traffic control checkpoint on one end of the bridge.

Everyone in Charlie Battery (except Phil and two other Marines) had prior crowd control and riot training when they were on USS *Trenton*, and then again, when they were on their field operation in Djibouti. Most had taken the Non-Lethal Weapons Course and knew how to set up a roadblock, stop traffic, and approach suspects and vice versa. When it came to approaching suspects, the Marines had been taught to have one Marine approach the suspect and have two or three other Marines standing back, providing cover. Their training included information on the possibility of suicide bombers, so they were very careful when performing their crowd control and checkpoint duties.

When it came to setting up roadblocks, they used traffic cones to funnel cars off to the side of the road where Marines would have them stop, and then ask passengers to get out of their car. They would search the men and boys on the spot, but out of respect for their privacy, they'd take the women and girls to a tent, where they'd be searched (patted down) privately. The Marines were mainly searching for weapons, but rarely found any. Phil recalls finding a few knives and handguns. What they found most often was cash—a lot of American and Iraqi currency—and hashish, which they apparently carried in chunks.

We'd talked among ourselves about if this duty was going to be like in Israel, where people got blown up daily.

LCpl. Phil Lubin

Searching the Iraqis was initially a tense duty for the Marines because of the uncertainty of how they would react and the very real possibility of suicide bombers doing their worst, as they do in Israel. After a few days of this duty, however, the tension seemed to wear off, and the Marines adjusted to their new assignment. There was a steady flow of traffic, and Charlie Battery settled into a simple rhythm of standing guard, and being off duty, while remaining in their area. Mail and packages were beginning to arrive regularly, and the war seemed to have been won. Then one day, a routine roadblock encounter made the war more personal for some of the Marines in Charlie Battery who were on duty at the time.

A Personal Encounter

Private Barr recalled that afternoon when a taxi drove up to the checkpoint. As usual, they asked the driver to get out of the vehicle and took him through the usual search routine. Then Barr noticed a wooden box that was strapped to the top of his taxi, and he motioned that he needed to check the box as well. The Iraqi driver became very upset and started objecting and gesturing his opposition, but since no one spoke his language, they did not know what he was saying.

His violent reaction to them searching the box made the Marines on duty even more suspicious of what was in it. So jumping up on the car, Barr pried open the top of the box. Inside was the dead body of a young girl; obviously, the man's daughter. The box was her coffin. Instantly, Barr understood what the Iraqi man had been trying to tell him and as best he could, Barr began to apologize. "I stopped searching coffin-size boxes that day. I don't know enough to follow the politics of the war, and whether or not we were right or wrong—but I do know it wasn't that little girl's fault. I think about her a lot."

Word of the incident spread rapidly through Charlie Battery, and the Marines relaxed their attitude towards the women and children as they came up to the checkpoint. "It wasn't like any of us spoke Arabic and could talk to these people," said Phil. "We just did the best we could."

> I eye-balled them as they came up to us. Mostly they looked like a bunch of pathetic people who needed our help.
>
> *LCpl. Joseph Turcotte*

Letters Home from Nasiriyah

Their duty under bridge gave the Marines time to write letters home, much to the delight of the families.

Letter from Doc Sanders to his daughter, Alli:

25 April 2003

Hey, Big-n. How are you doing? Keeping your chin up?! How's the dance classes going? Well, I hope you know that I love you and think about your smiling face all the time. Daddy misses you. Whenever you start to miss me and you wish I was there, go give momma a great big hug and tell her why, and I'm sure momma will cheer you up. Well I'm going to sleep for now. I love you! Keep your chin up and keep smiling.

Daddy

P.S. I love you.

Letter from Phil:

Nasiriyah, undated

What's up, Dad?

Right now I'm sitting on Nasiriyah's West Bridge because I'm guarding it. We have been made into a provisional rifle platoon because there is no more use for Arty [artillery]. It is hot and boring here. Two days ago, it was 114 degrees, and yesterday, it poured. The good thing is we put a sign out that says, "Marines will kill for food" and I guess the Army thinks we're serious, so they toss out all kinds of things when they drive by.

They're starting to talk about washdown and getting on the ship, and they told us we would be in Lejeune around June or July. I don't know if you've heard about the Marines shooting an RPG, but do I have a story for you. I gotta go, so I'll talk to you later.

Letter from Doc Sanders to his wife, Becky:

26 April 2003

Hey, Sweetheart,

Well I think the word is that we are going to be moving tomorrow. Which is a good thing as long as we are moving back south (back towards Kuwait). I can't wait to be home. This part of the military sucks. I've got to see some cool things, sick things, and the poverty level over here. I wish the mail system was better; that's the worst part. More phone calls would be better also. You don't need to worry about me, and I'll be home soon. So do you have the horseshoe pit set up yet? 40 feet apart. Time to stop for chow. Well, going to go for now, I love you all.

Mrs. Becky Sanders remembered how despondent she and her girls felt during this time because "Hank [Doc] had been gone three months, and the girls and I missed him terribly." Their oldest daughter, six-year-old Haley, kept every letter she received from her father under her pillow. Their youngest daughter, three-year-old Alli, got very sad at times. She would suddenly start crying and say, "I'm sad because I want my daddy." Becky recalls how Haley was her "rock." "When she would start to see me get sad, she would always come and hug me and tell me everything would be all right." The highlights of their week was when one of Doc's letters arrived. Becky recalls that she sent letters at least every other day. "Hank asked me to spray my perfume, White Diamonds, on the letters. He said he would sleep with the envelopes when I would remember to spray them."

Since the mail from Iraq was still taking three weeks to reach us back home, we had no idea of where Charlie Battery was located, or where they were about to go next.

> Hank asked me to spray my perfume on the letters. He said it gave him a little piece of home and me.
>
> *Becky Sanders, wife*

Remembering Those Who Fell

As April came to a close, Charlie Battery prepared to move further south. They were about to move out of Iraq, and back into Kuwait, by way of Camp Shoup. But before they left Nasiriyah, the battalion held a memorial service in honor of their three fallen Marines—1st Lt. Pokorney, CWO Arnold, and CWO Channel. During the morning of 28 April, they held their ceremony next to the northern bridge, which spanned the Saddam Canal. Appropriately, this was the bridge where 1st Lt. Pokorney was killed some seven weeks earlier.

During the past few days, the weather had been unbearably hot for the heavily burdened Marines. Phil and Noyes remembered that the temperatures were in the high 90s, with constantly blowing dust that kept the Marines gritty, grimy, and somewhat slimy to the touch. Today, however, was different.

1st Lt. Pokorney and 1st Lt. Ben Williams

> This morning was unusually cold, which perhaps mirrored the occasion. Today was a sunrise memorial service for 1st Lt. Frederick E. Pokorney. All of the 1/10 Staff was in attendance, along with most of the battalion. Faces were sullen, greetings were happy, but short . . . conversation was almost nil . . . .
>
> The ceremony was held 200 meters north of the Saddam Canal, next to the AAV that Fred and his men were in when they were attacked, that now sits on its side in a ditch. The tracks were unattached, and filled with mud, and a large exit wound resembling a huge sunflower could be seen in the side of the AAV; a testament to the explosive power of an RPG . . . . The 1st Sgt. formed us up around two smart-looking Marines holding the national ensign and the Marine Corps colors. Between the Marines

was a traditional pair of boots, heels together at a 45
degree angle, a rifle behind them with a bayonet inserted
into the ground, and a helmet on top.

The sight of this caused my throat to tighten, my teeth to
clench, and my eyes to tear .... [from the personal journal
of gunfire liaison Lt. John Doran, USN, a good friend of
1st Lt. Fred Pokorney]

Several Marines spoke at the ceremony. First Lieutenant Matt
Neely, who filled in admirably after 1st Lt. Pokorney was killed,
talked about the attack in which he died, and how the first two fire
missions 1st Lt. Pokorney called in had successfully silenced the
Iraqi fire. Colonel Glenn Starnes, CO of 1/10 spoke next. A
reserved man in public, Col. Starnes spoke in a voice which belied
the emotions that were bubbling to the surface. He talked about
how he regretted that he was unable to bring home every Marine
that he deployed, then he referred to his lieutenant as "a gentle
giant ... always with a smile on his face, and something nice to
say." Other Marines also spoke about 1st Lt. Pokorney in equally
complimentary manner, but the final word was left to the 1/10
chaplain, LT Kevin Norton, who read from the Book of Mark,
Chapter 13 "You will not know when the Master of the House
will call, but be ready."

As Lt. Col. Starnes conducted the memorial, the Marines
looked over the burnt-out AAV, and as sporadic automatic rifle fire
could be heard in the background, the Marines again understood
that Marines would continue to die in battle—no matter how hard
they trained or how well-prepared they were for their enemy.

"It made me angry all over again," Phil recalled later. "I didn't
know 1st Lt. Pokorney, but he was one of us. We sure got even
with the Iraqis afterwards. I'm sure they'll remember our eight
days of arty barrages for a long time."

And with that, the ceremony for 1/10's casualties was called
to a close. Phil, Czombos, Bechu, and all the Marines dispersed
quietly, holding their thoughts to themselves, as they readied
themselves for their next missions.

Return to Camp Shoup

The days had run together since they crossed the LoD into Iraq,
and the Marines had lost track of time. Even though many had
kept dairies and journals, like Charlie Battery's Cpl. Gault, most

couldn't tell you what the date was on any given day. They moved from town to town and they all began to look the same. Until finally, it was time to return to Camp Shoup.

The return to Camp Shoup was very different than their initial stay. Phil and few of his buddies had gotten trucked from Nasiriyah to Camp Shoup as part of an AP. They recalled the trip's relaxed attitude and how easy the journey went. When they arrived, the camp was being dismantled, and most of the tents were down. Since they got to the camp before the main force, they grabbed some of the few available racks, showered, slept, and ate. The best part of Shoup was that now it had real showers. At last, the contractors had finished building the camp, and Charlie Battery utilized the plumbing system to its fullest. Phil bragged that "We'd take two or three showers a day, just because we could." Lance Corporal Turcotte admitted that Camp Shoup was no "New York or Boston, but it had real kitchens by now, with real food and cold soda. I don't know if I'd call it nice, but it was much better than we'd experienced the past couple of months."

The remainder of Charlie Battery arrived at Camp Shoup a few days later, in late April. With the better part of the 7,000 Marines in Task Force Tarawa heading back out of Iraq, space was limited in the camp, and most of Charlie Battery just threw their sleeping bags on the sand and slept under the warm desert sky.

The problems and concerns of February and March were forgotten. They ignored the flies and accepted the scarabs, lizards, and dung beetles as a boring part of the landscape. But as Cpl. Delarosa said, "We didn't care. Nothing bothered us anymore. We were on our way out, and we knew we were on the way home."

Chapter 8

The Way Home

The Marines have set up all sorts of tours in Spain for us,
to go to museums and churches, but I think we're
all gonna skip that junk, and just
drink and get hammered.

*Email from a Charlie Battery Marine who has since matured and
would now prefer to remain anonymous*

**Kuwait Naval Base to USS
Ashland
4 May–22 June 2003**

I was checking my email on the morning of 12 May, when an email from Phil rolled in—he was alive! And not only that, he was even reachable! Quickly, I called his mother, Jamie, and gave her his email address, and then bragged to a few of my friends that I'd heard from him. It would be great to receive regular emails from him, and I hoped he'd be able to fill me in on some of the incidents he'd so briefly mentioned in his letters. And, of course, it was even better news that he was safely in Kuwait and scheduled to leave soon.

Phil and Charlie Battery began to arrive in Kuwait Naval Base on 4 May. With the fighting ceased, the Marine's biggest task now was to prepare their 7-tons, Humvees, and their 155s for wash-down and shipment back to Camp Lejeune. "I was AP from Shoup to Kuwait also," he said later. "They flew a few of us back by helicopter. That was fun! I came back with Lieutenants Shea, Warren, and Turcotte, and now we got to hang out on *Ashland*. They began to cycle us back in groups, to let us clean up and come back to the world. We had been in the field 96 days."

Corporal Czombos joined Phil about a week later when he and the rest of the main body of Charlie Battery arrived in Kuwait on board *Ashland*. "It was nice to get back on board. We'd been wearing the same clothes since we disembarked in January—we stank! At one point, we'd worn our MOPP suits for two weeks straight, and these things could stand up on their own."

Paul Czombos remembers the 7 May phone call when he finally believed his son had survived the war and was truly safe. "God, it was such a relief to hear his voice. He was back. He was safe, and he said that he had 20–25 hours of tapes, loads of pictures, and he'd be home in 5–6 weeks. I could live and breathe again."

Washdown Duty

Now that Charlie Battery was back in Kuwait, they had to inventory, repair, and clean their howitzers and their vehicles. Three months of humping through the rough desert terrain, the rain and sandstorms, as well as the battle of Nasiriyah had

Reloading heavy equipment into USS *Ashland*

taken a toll on the equipment, and although the maintenance troops had done wonders in keeping it in working order, now the vehicles had to be thoroughly checked out, repaired, and cleaned. At the end of the day, only one piece of rolling stock (a trailer), out of an initial total of 225, was not fixable.

"Washdown duty was a breeze," said Phil. "Every piece of equipment, every piece of rolling stock, had to be as disassembled as much as possible, and then thoroughly cleaned and washed. We used fire hoses to spray the equipment clean, as well as some sort of disinfectant." This was more than standard Marine Corps maintenance and sanitary standards; these cleanings and inspections were performed to the FDA standards. Within reason, military souvenirs were to be expected, but neither the Marine Corps nor the Food & Drug Administration wanted the dung beetles, camel killers, or any similar desert wildlife brought back to the United States.

Everyone in Charlie Battery loved washdown duty. Daytime temperatures were in the 100s, so what better way to cool off than dowsing themselves while performing their duties? Cpl. Gault recounted, "This was the Middle Eastern weather I remembered from Djibouti. So we soaked everything in sight, including ourselves—after all, we were supposed to clean our gear, right?" On top of staying cool and clean, Cpl. Goodson reminded me they were also getting packages from home, along with much of the mail that had accumulated over the past several weeks.

This was easy duty! We had clean clothes, real food, and regular email access.

Cpl. Ryan Gallagher

While I was unaware of their daily water fights and latest mail deluge, the almost-daily emails from Phil were a welcome change from the weeks of not hearing from him at all. The war news had trickled to a halt; most of the television news featured repetitive shots of the Saddam statue being pulled down in Baghdad, interviews with tired Marines, and yet more shots of waving and cheering Iraqi civilians.

As we parents enjoyed the increasing number of emails and phone calls with our sons, a few of the Charlie Battery wives received some very welcome news from their husbands too. Their husbands were coming home on an advanced party (AP) and would arrive well in advance of the main body of Task Force Tarawa. Christy Fontenoy and son, Cody, were one of the lucky families. Christy recalls, "We had John here almost a month before the main body. I had had a relatively easy pregnancy, but now I knew that he would be here for sure when our baby was born." (The Fontenoys' second child, son Dylan, was born on 30 June 2003.) Becky Sanders, who was also expecting a child, was equally surprised and relieved that Doc was flown home as part of the advance party. "The girls were just ecstatic, as was I, especially since he was here with me when our baby was born." (The Sanders' third child, Nicholas, was born 6 June 2003.)

Explosion on USS *Saipan*

The relative calm and relaxed atmosphere surrounding the Kuwait Naval Base was suddenly shattered one day with another accident. This accident, involving an explosion on board USS *Saipan*, cost the Marines eleven injured but, fortunately, no deaths. Back home, the news channels reported an explosion on USS *Saipan*, one of the amphibious assault ships of Task Force Tarawa. Instantly, the various networks, especially Fox, extrapolated the explosion to Saddam's revenge, or Al-Qaida operatives, and other equally sinister doings. Phil's mom, Jamie, called me, and asked if I thought the war had resumed, if Phil was safe, and so on. "He's fine," I told her. "The TV news is making something out of nothing—it's just some jarheads with a souvenir problem."

And it turned out I was right. The problem was that now all the young Marines were caught with their souvenirs, which included a whole arsenal of ammo, fuses, grenades and other military hardware meant to cause damage. When Phil called me from Spain later, when he was on liberty, he told me about the souvenir crisis after the accident on *Saipan*. "We'd all brought back some neat stuff, but when they had the explosion on *Saipan*, the Marine Corps went bullshit and searched everybody. They could have equipped a division with what they took off of us. I had some Iraqi .50 cal. tracer ammo and some Iraqi artillery fuses. Other guys had hand grenades, RPG rounds, AK-47s, handguns. It would have been a great Fourth of July if they hadn't taken all my stuff away."

On the other hand, Top Santivasci remembered the same incident and its subsequent repercussions far differently "A Marine in the Air Wing had picked up one of our DPICM bomblets, and tossed it in a trash can when they reembarked on *Saipan*. When it blew up, it not only injured him, but the blast blew up the berthing area on the other side of the bulkhead. What an idiot!" Gunny Lambert remembered the day also. "I'd warned them to keep their souvenirs sensible," he said. "But after the problem on *Saipan*, it was my job to shake them down. I took away RPG rounds, mortar fuses, artillery fuses, C4 plastic explosives, blasting caps, and a lot of Iraqi ammunition. I let them know how angry I was with them."

Corporal Aguila agreed that Gunny was pretty angry. "Oh man, it was a 2-day ass-chewing. When we woke up, he'd chew us out. At night, he'd chew us out again. During the day, every time they gave us a 'last chance' to give up our good stuff, then he'd find something else, and chew us out again. It's funnier now than it was then."

> I was pissed at what I found on them!
>
> *GySgt. Clay Lambert*

As Top Santivasci related the incident, his drill instructor persona began to resurface "I had no problem with the boys bringing back helmets, gas masks, and spent cartridges, but some of them just got stupid with what they tried to bring home. Things got so bad that someone even took some C4 explosives that fell off a truck. I mean, what do you do with C4—wait ten years and blow off your child's arm? We chewed their asses for that one, too."

When I was discussing this incident with Gunny Lambert after their return home, he proceeded to get irate again, pointing out, "Assuming they don't hurt themselves now, what happens in 15 or 20 years when their child or a grandson picks up this old shell, and it goes off? Then it's not so funny."

By 18 May, however, Top and Gunny had Charlie Battery disarmed and ready to ship out, as did the other senior NCOs for the 7,000 other Marines in Task Force Tarawa. With little fanfare in the harbor, each ship sounded its horn and sailed away for home.

Homeward Bound

Pulling out of the harbor was a quiet affair. Phil recalls that everyone realized they were on their home, but "I was too beat to celebrate." Corporal Czombos explained the relaxed attitude by noting, "I knew the Marine Corps would take care of us on the way home, and they probably wouldn't make us do anything difficult." Czombos was right; the Marine Corps let Charlie Battery decompress. While *Ashland*'s food had been good on the voyage to Kuwait, it was even better on their voyage home, or as Doc suggested, "maybe it was because we'd been living on MREs" and all the Charlie Battery Marines had to do was eat, sleep, and shower.

Even when *Ashland* had a breakdown in the Persian Gulf, the Marines weren't bothered. Charlie Battery watched movies and planned the parties and meals they would enjoy upon their return to America. Corporal Gault said, "We watched more action movies than I had ever imagined. Bruce Willis, Steven Seagal, you name it; we saw it." The Marine Corps obtained current movies for their troops, which was much appreciated.

Email from Phil:

25 May 2003

Go see the new Bruce Willis movie, "Tears of the Sun." It's really good. We're supposed to be in Cartegena, Spain on the 4, and stay until the 9, then be home by the 22. It's getting close and I can't wait. When you come down when I get back, it's dinner and drinks, followed by a stop at the tat parlor. Sounds like fun, huh!"

> **It was quiet on board when we left. We were tired. We were mentally beat.**
>
> *LCpl. Phil Lubin*

Entrance of the Suez Canal

Within a few days, however, *Ashland* was steaming past the Horn of Africa, rounding west past Yemen, and then heading north through the Red Sea towards the Suez Canal. By 31 May, they had reached the Suez Canal for an 0330 transit. Phil was back manning one of the ship's .50 caliber machine guns, which meant he was topside again as they traversed the canal. "Being on the security detail was great," he said later. "It took 18 hours to go through the Canal, and I got to see a little bit of Egypt this time also. We took security seriously, but we weren't nearly as edgy this time."

About this time, the Marine Corps threw a "steel beach party" for their troops on *Ashland*. A steel beach party is a shipboard party, held on the flight deck. Corporal Gault remembered the day fondly. "It was a great idea." Phil added, "It was an all-day party. They gave us a few beers. There was music; they ran a barbecue; and we could wear civvies, or what-ever we wanted." In addition to the food and the music, the Marine Corps provided golf clubs, and the Marines could tee-up off driving-range mats, and hit balls into the ocean. Corporal Czombos recalled the essential part of the party, as he commented on how "They only gave us two beers each. We would have drunk a lot more, which is probably why they limited us to two."

Their steel beach party

But there was a serious side to this slow-motion voyage back. In comparison to the Vietnam days, where the Marines were flown home, and then dumped in airports to fend for themselves, the Marine Corps was deliberately bringing their troops home slowly, so they could decompress and unwind before arriving back in the United States.

Reflections on "Their" War

While Chaps Ritchie was returning home on USS *Bataan*, instead of *Ashland* with Charlie Battery, his counseling and ministering activities continued, as did that of the other ministers, priests, and rabbis, on every ship in the convoy. The Marines had arranged to have counselors on board each of the ships, and each Marine soon discovered that he had mandatory debriefing classes to attend. Each counseling team was lead by a chaplain trained in critical stress debriefing.

While only time will tell if Phil, his friends, and the other Marines needed to take advantage of what the Marine Corps provided for them, most of Charlie Battery took the sessions somewhat nonchalantly. When asked about the sessions, Phil's attitude seemed to mirror that of others in his battery. "We had to sit with the counselors, and if we were bothered by seeing dead bodies or anything, they wanted us to talk to them about it. I was fine with what I'd done, so I just sat there." Corporals Gault and Czombos basically agreed with Phil, and additionally, each Marine pointed out that his war was much different than that of an infantry Marine. "We didn't see anything in the way of bodies," Czombos explained. "We're an arty battery, so we didn't see much of what we'd done."

> We're an arty battery, so we didn't see much of what we'd done.
>
> *Cpl. Michael Czombos*

Doc Sanders had a different take on his participation in the classes. "I was trained and ready to help my Marines, of course, and so I was a little disappointed I wasn't able to use my training. On the other hand, that meant that none of my friends had been hurt, so as I look back, that's a better thing."

While none of the Marines expected anyone in the civilian world to understand what they'd experienced in battle, some of them were surprised at the lack of knowledge at what they'd done, or even where they'd been. After he had returned to his home in Arkansas in June, and come back to Camp Lejeune in July, LCpl. Jones talked about how people responded to his war experiences, "I was asked so many times if I felt bad about what I'd done, or what I'd saw, or if I was a baby-killer, that I started wondering why I didn't feel bad. Then one day, I realized that I had no reason to feel bad—I hadn't done anything bad. I'd served the Marine Corps and my country—I'd done my job, and done it well. So screw them."

After returning to Youngstown, Ohio in July, Cpl. Czombos found the lack of knowledge and interest about the war puzzling. "For sure everyone was happy to see me when I got home," he recalled, "but no one remembered Nasiriyah. People thought the war was about Jessica Lynch or Baghdad, and no one knew what we'd done." Corporal Delarosa received the same reaction from his friends and family in Tampa, Florida. "We kicked butt in Nasiriyah," he said. "But no one seemed to know anything about it." Phil confirmed these observations. "Nasiriyah was the biggest battle of the war, and almost nobody knows or cares very much about it. Well, the Iraqis and us all know about it."

> Nasiriyah was the biggest battle of the war and no one back home remembered it.
>
> *Cpl. Jorge Delarosa*

Three-Day Liberty in Spain

As *Ashland* steamed back through the Mediterranean Sea, Phil and the others all relaxed and decompressed. While they all looked forward to returning home, the Marine Corps also gave them a small, but much-appreciated bonus: they had been granted a three-day liberty on the voyage home. Each of the ships in the convoy was scheduled to stop in a separate Portuguese or Spanish port on the voyage home; *Ashland* was due to stop in Cartegena, Spain.

Phil and I emailed each other daily, and even though we had nothing of specific importance to say, it was just nice to see a paragraph from him in the morning when I dialed up my ISP. Mostly he expressed his enthusiasm for his upcoming liberty in Cartegena, and he gave me a daily update of *Ashland*'s expected arrival date back in Morehead City.

Ashland docked in Cartegena on 5 June and unleashed its cargo of Marines on the unwary city. They were in port for four days, of which every Marine was required to spend one day on guard duty. Charlie Battery's plan, however, was to beeline for the nearest open bar, regardless of the hour, and then look to

> Oh, it was an awesome three days. We got so smashed!
>
> *LCpl. Phil Lubin*

Phil in Cartegena, Spain

Lamb, Phil, and Barr in Cartegena, Spain

Phil and friends with some young ladies

introduce themselves to any women fortunate enough to cross their paths. Phil recalled this liberty fondly. "There was this bar that was open in the morning, and we started the day drinking tequilas, then beer, and then we just drank whatever bottle we recognized." Corporal Czombos reveled in the Spanish food. "God, we had some amazing meals! I remember a steak we had at one restaurant that had to be the best steak I'd ever eaten. Cartegena? I just don't remember much else."

To make these sojourns into the city, the Marines were required to sign off and on the ship, and they could not go out by themselves. They had to have at least one other Marine with them. Phil and LCpl. Jones went off one day, and then Pvt. Barr and LCpl. Lamb joined them later. "We worked on scotch, on whiskey, and also some Jaegermeister," Lamb said. "The Spanish beer was great, especially since we'd drunk nothing but soda on shipboard, and bottled water in the desert for the past four months." Alcohol wasn't the only attraction in Spain that captured the Marine's attention. The Spanish ladies played a huge role in how the Marines enjoyed their time in port as well. Jones and Lamb admired the Spanish ladies they met. "They were all gorgeous, and since Lubin can almost play the guitar, we told them we were rock and roll singers, which they believed for a while. But then, being drunk, we told them we were Marines, and they still stuck around."

What Marine Command did not realize, however, was that 1/10 would suffer more Marines injured in Cartegena than in Nasiriyah. "We saw these Spanish kids with skateboards," said Phil. "So we went over to them, told them we were skateboard pros, and took their boards. I was skating fine, despite maybe having had a few beers, until I fell off a rail, and dislocated my elbow." Two other Marines also hurt themselves skateboarding and were carried back to *Ashland*. Phil's elbow was bent 180 degrees the wrong way, so "six Marines held me down, and they snapped my arm back into place. Nothing in my life ever hurt as bad as that!"

Phil and Jones with a local admirer

When he called me on 7 June from Spain, of course, I was happy to hear from him. Then he told me about the drinking and his skating injury. I alternated between being amused and pretending to be a disgusted father, but basically, so long as he was neither disfigured, permanently injured, or under arrest, I just wanted him to have the best time possible. "Try to take some pictures," I told him, "and please try not to do anything irrevocably stupid."

Their officers and senior NCOs were more restrained in their festivities. "We found an Irish pub," 1st Lt. Shea said, "and we hung out and drank beer and relaxed. And we called our wives a lot."

The Home Stretch

On 8 June, *Ashland* pulled out of Cartegena and rejoined the convoy home. The Marines continued to decompress on shipboard by simply eating, sleeping and watching movies. To break up that routine, Cpl. Gault explained, "For variety, we'd go topside, smoke, and just bullshit with each other. It was an easy voyage home." Lance Corporal Bechu recalled it the same way. "We just relaxed. We had email access this time, so I emailed Laura a lot. Otherwise, I just didn't do much of anything."

Phil on board ship at the "morale" station

Down to one working arm, Phil watched movies and spent time reading, as they still had some two weeks at sea before they landed back in Morehead City. But having spent the weeks prior to Cartegena in the same routine, boredom set in quickly, so again, the Marines improvised. "I was a Virginia chess champion," LCpl. Lamb said, "so I taught a couple of my friends how to play. Lubin wasn't half-bad, once he remembered which piece was which. It was actually amazing at how well some of the others could play, once they decided to concentrate."

Back on land, Becky Sanders, Leah Starner, Paul Czombos, Royce and Sharon Goodson—and all the other parents, spouses, and girlfriends—planned our trips to Camp Lejeune. As the actual ETA of *Ashland* changed, we booked and re-booked our hotel rooms, and counted down the days until June 21, or 22, or 23, when the Marines of Charlie Battery were actually going to return.

Chapter 9

Return to Camp Lejeune

I left on January 14 with 55 Marines,
And on June 22 I brought all
55 Marines back home.

1st Lt. Sean Shea,
Executive Officer, Charlie Battery, 1st Battalion, Tenth Marines

Camp Lejeune, NC
22 June 2003

The drive south that day was certainly a lot more enjoyable than my previous trip to see Phil off back in January.

Phil had warned me that email service would stop when they were a day or so off the coast. While I'd gotten accustomed to the almost-daily email contact, I certainly understood they had to get the ship and gear squared away for unloading, so I didn't mind not hearing from him for those few days.

My son was alive; he was healthy; and in his emails, he'd expressed an urgent interest in beer and yet another tattoo (at least I understood the beer part). What a great day it was going to be! Even more so because Phil didn't know I was bringing his best friend, Matt Wright, with me, as a surprise for him.

Matt and I left Pennsylvania at 0300. Since the Marine Corps had to unload and bus some 7,000 Marines off seven ships at Morehead City, they could not give us an exact time as to when Charlie Battery would be on base and released. In any event, I decided it was best to leave early—there was no way that I'd break my January promise to Phil to be there when he came back because I was stuck in traffic, or some other such inexcusable reason.

Phil called us when we were just driving through Baltimore (coincidentally at almost the exact spot where I'd seen USS *Hope* on my January trip). But the mood that fine June day was far brighter—he was telling me *Ashland* was currently moored off Onslow Beach, and they were discharging the tanks and other vehicles onto the beach via the LCACs. He also said he couldn't reach Matt, and then he asked me if I had his cell number? I told him I thought Matt had gone off with his girlfriend for the weekend, but that I'd try to track him down. I reminded Phil to call his mom (who was in on the surprise), and the connection died as we went through a tunnel.

Phil and I talked again several times during the morning. There was nothing special to say; I think we both just liked to have the ability again to pick up the phone and talk. Perhaps it was the beginning of his return to normalcy, or mine ... whatever it was, it was just nice to be able to have a conversation with him again.

The miles were flying by on this trip, and we cruised into Jacksonville in the very early afternoon. Although Charlie Battery was scheduled to be released at approximately 1500, I told Matt we needed to go on base right away. We couldn't stop at the hotel or for food; we had to go immediately to his barracks. There was no reason for us to be there so early, but I had this incredibly strong feeling that my proper place was on the base, waiting for him.

I also warned Matt that my taste in music was going to rule for the day, and I cranked up one of my Scottish bagpipe CDs. My father, Phil's grandfather, played the pipes, and I couldn't think of any music more appropriate to welcome Phil home.

The Marine Corps had mailed all off-base family members a special "Homecoming" sticker to put in their windshields in order for them to enter the base. After checking my ID against Phil's name on their list, the Marine guard reached into the car and shook my hand. "He's back, Sir, and he's safe," the Marine said. "Congratulations, and welcome aboard." Dear God, it's true, I thought.

There was quite a crowd already gathered at their barracks, at their release point, so I wasn't the only anxious and excited family member that afternoon. Having seen where Charlie Battery would be released helped calm me down, and after Matt and I walked around a little, we got back in the car, and checked into the Microtel.

On the off-chance that I might meet any of Phil's NCOs or officers, I took a few minutes and went to one of the many barbershops situated on the road leading into Camp Lejeune and got a trim. Did I need one? Not by civilian standards, but I wanted everything, including my own appearance, to be as perfect as possible. Unnecessary? Absolutely, but I wanted this day, and everything involved in it, to be as perfect for him as possible.

The Marine Corps had given each battalion some money, and the Marines and Key Volunteers of 1/10 had gone to great lengths to create a very festive, circus-like atmosphere. They'd put up party tents, brought in clowns and face-painters, hired a DJ, and had pizza delivered throughout the afternoon. Headquarters Building was festooned with banners hanging from the windows, as well as signs stuck in the grass. Families sat at the tables under the tents and talked about their sons while children played on the old 105mm cannon sited on the HQ lawn. Spouses and fathers chatted with strangers holding signs saying something like "NJ welcomes back ....." This in turn would inspire someone to inquire, "I'm from Jersey too. Who's your son?"

Headquarters building sign

Even the cars and vans in the parking lots were decorated; minus the tin cans you see tied onto a car at a wedding, you could almost read 1/10 history's off the windows: "Charlie Battery kicked butt in Nasiriyah!" "Bravo—Kings of Battle!" "Ohio Loves Alpha Battery!" "Task Force Tarawa!" and so forth. Nearly everyone seemed to be holding American flags, Marine Corps flags, and individual signs. Mine was simple. Like an election sign, it was just a giant piece of oak tag with a long, wooden handle that read, "LCpl. Phil!" He'd see it.

But as the music played through the afternoon, and the clowns and face-painters circulated to keep the children happy, we kept checking the Status Board. Charlie Battery's ETA kept sliding back 30–45 minutes at a clip. The Marine supervisors and Key Volunteers talked to the adults and tried their best to keep everyone informed. Everyone took the news with good grace; after all, we couldn't do anything to speed things up. The Key Volunteers and wives who planned the party—Lisa Santivasci, Jamie Lambert, Christy Fontenoy, Becky Sanders, and Amanda Aguila—were as anxious to see their husbands as we were to see our sons.

Several false alarms sounded for the Charlie Battery families as small columns of Humvees drove down N Street

Headquarters building with welcome home signs

C Company marching in to be released to their families

with their horns blaring, filled with cheering and waving Marines, but as they drove past without stopping, we stopped waving and drifted back to the tents. At one point, two busses of Marines pulled up in our parking lot, and parents, children, and family ran to see who was arriving. They were from another section of 1/10, and as the men bounded off their busses, they were enthusiastically greeted by their families, and then they quickly disappeared out of the parking lot and into their barracks.

The afternoon passed; it was 1830, and most of the talk had ceased. Each family had broken up into its own small group; the children had long since stopped running around, and the infants were sleeping. The heat had even gone out of the June North Carolina sun, and we were resigned to Charlie Battery being the last group to be released. And then, two 7-ton trucks growled up next to HQ Building, and a few Marines began to throw down and stack gear on the grass. Another father and I went over and asked them, "Whose gear? What unit?" "Charlie Battery, Sir," one Marine answered, and the other father turned around, cupped his hands to his mouth and hollered, "It's them!"

As the crowd got up and began to move over to where the gear was being laid out in neat rows on the grass, two more busses pulled up behind HQ Building, and the Marines began to disembark. But instead of running madly to the crowd as the other

Marine units had done, Charlie Battery formed up, dressed ranks, and marched over to us, with SSgt. Green counting cadence as they finished the last 100 yards of their incredible journey.

There was desultory clapping as they began to march towards us; it was as if no one knew what to do. Fuck that! I knew what to do, and I began to shout, "Ooh-rah, Charlie Battery! Way to go! Way to go Marines!" With one father yelling, the crowd quickly erupted, and all the other waiting fathers, mothers, wives and children shrieked and shouted and clapped as Charlie Battery marched towards us. As they halted in front of us, SSgt. Green barked an order, "Left, Face!" and they turned in unison towards us.

Whatever command or parting statement 1st Sgt. Winstead made was lost in the crowd's cheering, and as he dismissed his men, we began running and walking towards them, and the Marines broke ranks to meet us.

I found Phil easily as he walked towards me. He was far more tanned than when I'd left him in January, and wearing his green cammis and boondockers, he seemed to have grown taller. We stood in front of each other, and again, both of us seemed to be at a loss for words. "Welcome home, Phil," I said quietly, as I shook his hand and reached for him, "It's good to have you back."

LCpls. Rob Kranz and Phil Lubin return safely

Phil with Humvee back at Camp Lejeune

Chapter 10

Where Are They Now?

Spring 2004

Leading men in combat like those Marines in Battery C, and all of 1/10, was the greatest thing I have ever done. They performed their duties without failure.

Colonel Glen Starnes, Commanding Officer 1/10[16]

All good things come to an end, and Charlie Battery began breaking up in December 2003. Marines enlist. Marines get transferred to different units. Marines leave after they complete their four-year tours. In a typical year, there is a turnover of some 40,000 Marines in and out of the Marine Corps. But there is one constant: Marines keep training.

In January 2004, the remaining Charlie Battery Marines—Aguila, Bechu, Czombos, Gallagher Jones, Turcotte, Warren and Sanders—all left Camp Lejeune for a month of cold-weather training in California's Sierra Nevada Mountains, followed by two weeks of extreme cold-weather training in Minnesota. From the 110-degree heat of Iraq to the minus-55 degree winds of the Sierra Nevadas, these Marines are living examples of the line in the Marine's hymn, "in every clime and place." Because of the current political and military situation in Iraq, Charlie Battery is due to return to Iraq some time in April 2004, and this may be an opportunity for some of the Marines who are still with the unit to advance their careers. However, because of the current military and political situation in Iraq, the most probable next "clime and place" will be the Sunni Triangle.

Corporal Gaspar Aguila

Gaspar and Amanda Aguila

Corporal Aguila gets out of the Marine Corps in Autumn 2004, and he and his wife, Amanda, will return home to Portland, Oregon.

Private Paul Barr

Always a free-spirited individual, Pvt. Barr also decided to leave the Marines Corps, destination unknown.

Lance Corporal Sobola Bechu

Lance Corporal Bechu, still a Charlie Battery Marine, was promoted to corporal in November 2003. He has just volunteered to return to Iraq, and he will be shipping out again in September 2004. Additionally, he and Laura are now engaged to be married.

Sobola and Laura Bechu

Corporal Mike Czombos

Corporal Czombos, one of the few of the group still left in Charlie Battery, has about a year left in the Marines. Short of a transfer, he should also be back in Iraq in September.

Corporal Jorge Delarosa

Corporal Delarosa left the Marines Corps in December 2003 and returned home to Tampa, Florida. "It's nice to see my friends and family," he said, "but it's getting sort of boring. Also, it's like I don't quite fit in. They don't know or care what I've done, and I don't relate to things here. My friends back in Camp Lejeune keep telling me I should come back. I might just do that; I miss them."

Corporal Ryan Gallagher

Transferred to Alpha Battery, Cpl. Gallagher's four years are up in the summer of 2004. He is considering extending, and may well sign up for another tour.

Corporal Chris Gault

Corporal Gault's four-year enlistment in the Marine Corps finished in November 2003, and he headed for Houston, Texas with a Marine buddy to try his hand in the oil-field business. "Why not go now?" he told me. "My friend's father has some connections, so if I can get on a drilling rig, I can make a lot of money, so why not give it a shot?"

Chris Gault

Corporal Geoffrey Goodson

Corporal Goodson has another year with the Marines and remains committed to advancing himself as transfers and opportunities occur.

Cory Hebert and fiancée Leah

Corporal Cory Hebert

Corporal Hebert is engaged to Leah Starner, and they are due to be married on 10 July 2004. Additionally, he has volunteered to go back to Iraq, as he says, "There are Marines still fighting and dying in Iraq, and I don't feel right not being with them."

Lance Corporal Joshua Jones

Lance Corporal Jones was also transferred to Alpha Battery. His four years are up in the summer of 2004, and is considering extending his tour for another six months, where he may very well may find himself back in Iraq before the year's end.

Lance Corporal Nicholas Lamb

Lance Corporal Lamb didn't re-enlist, and in December 2003, he headed back to his home in Portsmouth, Virginia with plans to attend college.

Joshua Jones

Lance Corporal Phil Lubin

Phil was transferred to Bravo Battery, which was scheduled to go on a float with the 24th MEU in August 2004. In between trips to the Persian Gulf, he was on alert March 2004 as the 24th MEU was on standby for quick deployment to Haiti. Since it took only some 400 Marines to defuse that particular crisis, he and his new friends in Bravo Battery continued their joint infantry-artillery-armor training in preparation for returning to the Persian Gulf.

"I'm getting to know the Bravo guys," he said. "And I know they're all good Marines. But I still like to hang out with my friends from Charlie Battery; we all went through a lot together. Going off on a float should be pretty interesting, especially if we get to stop and visit Malta, Bahrain, and some of the other typical float ports of call. However, in the past several month's we've been getting a lot of urban training, and riot control work, so maybe that means we'll be heading out directly for Iraq or Afghanistan."

On 5 May 2004, the MEU was ordered to be ready for an immediate return to Iraq, and he expects to be flown back to Iraq in early July 2004.

Phil Lubin

Corporal Justin Noyes

Corporal Noyes re-enlisted for another four years and was promoted to sergeant. Additionally, he requested a transfer to EOD (explosive ordinance disposal), which will transfer him to Camp Pendleton, California. Currently, he is attending EOD training in Florida.

Petty Officer 3rd Class James "Doc" Sanders

Doc Sanders has a promising medical career in front of him should he stay in the U.S. Navy. Transferred out of Charlie Battery into Alpha Battery, he is currently studying to become a bio med technician, which will keep him in the Navy for an additional four years. "But I'll be in a non-deployable unit," he said, "so I can stay close to Becky and the children. And who knows what the opportunities will be in four years in either the Navy or the civilian world? I've worked hard; I'll be good to go either way."

Doc Sanders and family

Corporal Joshua Souza

Corporal Souza got out in March 2004, and returned to Worcester, Massachusetts, where he plans to go to college.

Lance Corporal Joseph Turcotte

Lance Corporal Turcotte got out in March 2004 and has definite career plans. "I got out because the BS wore me out, and I just didn't see the point in going through four more years of it. But I've got my Montgomery GI Bill money, and I plan to use it—I'm going to the University of New Hampshire and get a degree in history or literature, and then get a job teaching."

Lance Corporal Carl Warren

Lance Corporal Warren mustered out in April and plans to attend college at Towson State. "I do want to go to college," he said, "My dad always wanted me to go to college, and now I'm ready to go. Even though he saw me finish Parris Island and become a Marine, I wish he were here to see me finish school."

Carl Warren

Career Marines

First Lieutenant Sean Shea, Chaps Ritchie, MSgt. Michael Santivasci, GySgt. Clay Lambert, and SSgt. John Fontenoy are all career Marines, and they will do what the Marine Corps requires of them.

Michael Santivasci and family

John Fontenoy and family

First Lieutenant Shea was transferred to HQ Battery, where he is now the battalion logistics officer. He expects to be transferred again to the Marine Barracks in Washington, DC, where he is expecting a promotion to captain.

Chaps Ritchie accompanied his Charlie Battery Marines to Bridgeport and Minnesota. "Like I told you," he said, "I minister to the troops. It's really very simple—where they go, I go."

Top Santivasci and Gunny Lambert spend their hours getting their 1/10 and Charlie Battery Marines ready for the next float, for an emergency deployment to Haiti, or to go back to Iraq.

Staff Sergeant Fontenoy received a well-deserved promotion to Gunnery Sergeant, as well as a Meritorious Service Commendation for his exemplary efforts in Iraq.

Being a Marine

Careers and tours can range from the wildly exciting to the incredibly mundane as the vagaries of international politics and crises come into play. Even as the Marine units came back from Iraq, USS *Kearsarge* was detoured from her homeward-bound leg to the Liberian coast, should Marines have been needed to rescue American civilians. While those particular Marines may have thought that they were receiving too much action, most Marines joined the Corps in hopes of excitement, travel, and career opportunities, and they have generally had their wishes granted.

Since Desert Shield and Desert Storm in 1990 and 1991, Marines have been sent to Macedonia, Haiti, Liberia, Kosovo, the Balkans, Iraq, and recently, back to Haiti. Even in an-unexciting career, a Marine might be stationed in Korea, Okinawa, Bahrain, or various other international locations—not a bad background for a 22- or 23-year-old to have as the start to his or her career in the business world.

Regardless of being either a career Marine, or a one-tour enlisted man, they all carry one unifying distinction that few others in the world can claim—the title, "United States Marine."

Chapter 11

Afterword

There is only one story in the world today, and it's called Iraq. We have to get this right. If we get it right, many, many good things will flow from that for America, the world, and the Middle East. If we get it wrong, the world will not be a safe place for Americans. It will be a very dangerous place.

Thomas Friedman, "IMUS Show" interview
19 August 2003

May 2004

They're all home now. Phil and his friends in Charlie Battery returned in June 2003 safe and secure in the knowledge that their efforts in An Nasiriyah enabled the 1st MEF and the Army to capture Baghdad with far fewer casualties than anyone expected.

But Iraq is a country that has seen dozens of conquerors come and go, and as our administration ignored the history of the region, the war was seen by many to be spiraling out control as 2004 progressed. In April 2004 alone, we suffered more deaths than all the combat deaths of February through April 2003 combined (135 versus 65), and the administration's heavy-handed, Ahmed Chalabi and Halliburton-friendly policies managed to do something that no one else was able to do: unite the Sunnis and Shiites in opposition to our continued occupation of their country.

As we sit and watch the daily carnage and deaths of our Marines and soldiers being reported from Iraq, the hostage-takings, the murders of coalition diplomats and engineers from Spain, Korea, and Japan, and recent attacks on the oil rigs in the Gulf, the news just seems to get worse and worse.

The April 2004 uprising in Fallujah and the other Iraqi cities took the Bush administration by surprise. For all the talk of bringing a Jeffersonian democracy to Iraq, to date, there is not even a clear understanding in America as to why we initially went to war, and many of the parents, wives, and interested Americans would like to have the administration articulate a reason why our sons and husbands shipped out last year, and why most of them are shipping out again.

But lacking such an explanation from President Bush, perhaps it is worth remembering Tom Friedman's stunning 4 June 2003 column on *The New York Times* Op Ed page "Because We Could," in which he justified America's invasion of Iraq. Friedman wrote that we needed to hurt someone in the Arab world because of 9/11: we needed to show the Arab world that flying planes into office buildings was no longer acceptable, that suicide bombers on busses was unacceptable ... that their Muslim politics of hate were no longer acceptable—and that we would willingly take casualties in order to show them that this was no longer acceptable to us in the West.[17]

The most important point in Mr. Friedman's article was his follow-on thesis that Saddam Hussein, per se, was unimportant— that our invasion was merely an object lesson for the Arab world. As correct and succinct as Mr. Friedman usually is, it was still my son and his friends being sent to Iraq as the tip of our spear.

Marines are an unusual group. They go where they are sent, without complaint, and they do a thorough job when they get to their destination. Unlike the Army's 507th, whose fighting ability so emboldened the Iraqis in An Nasiriyah, or the prison guards in the Abu Ghraib prison scandals, Marines take their training seriously and fulfill their missions. And the parents and wives of Marines know this; the pride they feel in their Marine is balanced by the worry of what they know he is expected to accomplish— and to the lengths he will go to accomplish his mission.

It would be a relief to see their efforts, patriotism, and professionalism matched by those civilian leaders in authority. If we are told that "failure is not an option," then we'd like to see a coherent mission statement for Operation Iraqi Freedom to make it so.

This should best come from the Bush administration, especially since on 5 May 2004 they announced their intention to send fresh troops back to Iraq. This will include Phil, as part of the 24th MEU, as well as his remaining friends in Charlie Battery. As a parent, I'm not happy. But as the parent of a Marine, then by God, they're sending the best—but let the Marines clean this mess up their way.

But instead of the Bush administration's announcement, the game plan comes from writers like Tom Friedman, or former Marines like General Anthony Zinni. In a September 2003 speech at the Marine Corps Association Forum, General Zinni described the situation in which our troops currently find themselves. "You're dealing with the Jihads that are coming in to raise hell," he told the audience. "Crime on the streets that's rampant, ex-Ba'athists that are still running around, and the potential now for this country to fragment: Shi'ia on Shi'ia, Shi'ia on Sunni, Kurd on Turkomen. It's a powder keg."[18]

General Zinni is no stranger to this part of the world; he spent 15 years in the region, and in his last four years was the regional commander-in-chief. With such a unique background, he is eminently qualified to speak as an expert in American military operations in the Middle East. "We have got an entire region of the world that is chaotic and in turmoil," he continued, "and we have just seen the beginning of it. For decades more, we're going to be dealing with this problem. You're going to be fighting terrorists, you're going to be fighting against failed or incapable states that are sanctuaries for problems."[19]

This is a far different war than the one Phil and his fellow Marines experienced back in An Nasiriyah. Despite the confusion and the fog of war that reigned in their March 2003 battle, at least Lt. Col. Starnes, Lt. Col. Grabowski, the other officers, NCOs and enlisted men in 1/10 & 1/2, and the other units in RCT-2 knew their goal was to seize the bridges and secure the city and the highways in order to keep the convoys running north. That clarity of responsibility and mission seems to be missing now.

Despite the December 2003 capture of Saddam Hussein, Iraq now appears to be attracting every Western or U.S.-hating Arab extremist who wants to 'liberate' Iraq from Western influence. After the August 2003 bombing of the Baghdad UN headquarters, three groups took credit—yet only one was local—another was Hamas-Palestinian related, and the third was an Al-Qaida-related group.

It seems the Bush team has managed to create the very monster they claimed already existed: On 16 August 2003, the *Financial Times* quoted a Saudi Arabian minister who mentioned that "up to 3,000 Saudi men have gone missing in the Kingdom in two months"[20] When one remembers that 19 of the 9/11 terrorists came from Saudi Arabia, it doesn't take a brain surgeon to figure out they're drifting across that big open border into Iraq, and any American, Brit, or Western aid worker they come across is their target of opportunity—ask Nick Berg's parents.

Suddenly, Al-Qaida is back in the news. While they spent the second half of 2003 bombing targets in Morocco, Jordan, and Saudi Arabia, these targets in the Middle East rarely interested most Americans. However, the brutal railway bombing in Madrid, Spain in March 2004 brought Al-Qaida and Osama bin-Laden back to American interest and prominence.

Does the Al-Qaida threat to America remain?

Absolutely, but Al-Qaida is no longer a trendy problem unless it pertains to the administration's recent claims that Al-Qaida is now operating out of Iraq, or to slam the Democrats in a campaign speech. Unless Al-Qaida launches another successful terror attack on American soil, we won't know for sure about any danger from them until our Marines get another deployment order; for Kabul, the Northwest Frontier, or back to Iraq.

Even before the 5 May announcement, the Marines were being quietly returned to the Middle Eastern battlefields; as long ago as 22 November 2003, the Marines of Infantry Battalion 2/8 (the same Marines Phil and Charlie Battery supported with their artillery fire back in An Nasiriyah) were airlifted out of Camp Lejeune in the dead of night, and sent to Afghanistan. While the administration is trumpeting the stories of the troops coming home, it would have been more fair to the parents and wives of 2/8 had CNN cameras watched as their Marines shipped out at 0200 on that chilly November night.

The war has taken an ugly turn. In March and April 2003, Bechu, Lubin, Turcotte, Barr, Hebert, Delarosa, and the others were all greeted as liberators. But as the temperatures that summer reached 135 degrees, they were considered occupiers—there were far fewer jobs, much less electricity, gasoline rationing, and far more bloodshed now than before the war. As these problems play into the hands of the Arab extremists, the Iraq silent majority (the ones who cheered Charlie Battery in Al-Kut and Numiniyah) continue to worry about jobs, money, and medicine for their families. Our Marine liberators have morphed into Army occupiers, and the average Iraqi is too unemployed and worried about security to differentiate between the two or no longer cares.

At the same time, Iraqi domestic politics continue, totally confused, as the three main players debate on how they can best trump each other in their goal to take power. As the administration continues to tout America's role in bringing democracy to the Iraqi people, Iraqi local politics is a mix of Kurds, Sunnis, and Shiites—all of whom have loathed each other for centuries. The upcoming June 2004 vote for a provisional government should be most interesting.

Both the religious Iraqis and secular Iraqis, as well as the various Saudi, Sudanese, and Syrian Fedayeen understand the stakes at play here: if the United States' ideas and values triumph, we win more than Iraq. We will prevail in the entire Middle East. On the other hand, if the United States leaves prematurely, or is driven out of Iraq, then the extremists have won and will accurately claim their values and moral strength have prevailed over ours, and Charlie Battery's efforts will have been in vain.

But while this book is not written to discuss international politics or the administration's latest nation-building scheme, the parents and wives of our Marines know the politics and the problems all too well, for example, the lack of individual flak jackets and body armor for the troops. The fact is the Army decided several years ago (but after Desert Storm and Kosovo) that Humvees did not need to be armored. How many hundreds of Operation Iraqi Freedom soldiers have died because of this mistake? Entire towns are contributing financially to have their local Reserve and Guard Humvees armored. What a disgraceful turn of events. As the administration and the various Democratic and Republican candidates pursue their various political and military theories, it is worth remembering these policies and experiments are being vetted in the blood and sacrifice of our troops.

It was these Marines in Charlie Battery—Phil, Doc Sanders, Chris Gault, Mike Czombos, Cory Hebert, and all the other young Marines—with their varied reasons for joining the Marine Corps, who so successfully laid the groundwork for this important confrontation. Let's hope that our country has the same strength of will and fortitude as our sons and husbands in Charlie Battery.

What we want to celebrate and what we want to commemorate in this book is how our Marines of Charlie Battery—our sons, husbands, fathers, and boyfriends—trained, fought, and won in the expected historic Marine tradition. And like 1st Lt. Shea so proudly claimed: how they all came back home.

Welcome back, gentleman, and our congratulations on a job well done. Semper Fi.

Notes

Chapter 3

1. Robert Asprey, *At Belleau Wood*, 344.
2. *Ibid.*

Chapter 4

3. U.S. Marine Corps website, 15 Mar 2003.

Chapter 5

4. *The New York Times*, 13 Sept 2001, Op Ed.

Chapter 6

5. William Manchester, *Goodbye Darkness*, 391.
6. 1/10 Command Action Summary, 8 & 15.
7. *Ibid.*, 9 & 16.
8. *Ibid.*
9. *Ibid.*

Chapter 7

10. *Small Wars Manual*, 1940, 9.
11. *The New York Times*, 8 April 2003, B-8.
12. *The New York Times*, 9 April 2003, B-10.
13. *The New York Times*, 11 April 2003, 1.
14. *Ibid.*, B-6.
15. *Small Wars Manual*, 1940, 32.

Chapter 10

16. Friedman, interview, Imus Show, WFAN-AM, 19 Aug 2003.

Chapter 11

17. *The New York Times*, 4 June 2003, Op Ed.

18. Gen. Anthony Zinni, speech to the Marine Corps Association, 4 Sept 2003.

19. *Ibid.*

20. *The New York Times*, 16 Aug 2003, Op Ed.

Works Consulted

1st MEF Action Summary of Operation Iraqi Freedom.

Doran, Lt. John (USN). Personal Action Diary. Jan–June 2003.

Santivasci, MSgt. Michael. Personal Action Diary. Jan–June 2003.

USMC After-Action Report 1/10.

USMC After-Action Report 2/8.

USMC After-Action Report 3/2.

Glossary

0811. The MOS (military occupational specialty) designating an artilleryman.

7-ton. An abbreviation for the heavy trucks used by the Marines, which describes their cargo capacity of cargo and/or Marines.

AF East (Assault Force East). The seven ships comprising the convoy carrying the Marines of Task Force Tarawa to Kuwait.

AAV (amphibious assault vehicle). A tracked vehicle that typically carries Marines from their ship to the beach. It was used in OIF to carry Marines from Kuwait to Baghdad. Primarily used by the Marines.

APC (armored personnel carrier). An armored tracked vehicle that carries soldiers. Primarily used by the Army.

Berms. The huge sand walls delineating the border between Kuwait and Iraq.

CFF (call for fire) mission. When the forward observers call fire missions back to the command post.

Cammies. An abbreviation for camouflage clothing.

Code Red Mission. An artillery mission in which the guns fire in a timed manner at a pre-determined target in order to protect their own troops or trucks. In WWI and WWII, this was known as a "rolling barrage."

Condition 1. The state of carrying an M16 with a round (bullet) in the chamber, safety on, but otherwise, ready to fire.

Cutting squares. Marine term for sailing in a big grid square while on a float.

Desert Wedge. A specific formation in which the LAVs, 7-tons, tanks, and other vehicles are driven through the desert.

DPICM (dual-purpose improved conventional munitions). This is the basic type of shell fired by the M198 155mm howitzer.

EPW. Enemy prisoner of war.

FFE (fire for effect) Mission. A rapid-fire artillery mission where all the guns fire at one target.

Float. A Marine term relating to a six-month mission whereby the MEU "floats" to a variety of destinations, either for training or to be used in a variety of real-time missions (as when USS *Kearsarge* was dispatched to Liberia in order to rescue Americans and other Westerners trapped in the American embassy).

FO (forward observer). The Marine who is attached with, or is organic to, a forward maneuver unit who coordinates, directs, and observes the indirect fire of the artillery or mortar batteries. The 81mm mortar or artillery battery normally provides one to three individuals to observe and adjust the fires of the requesting unit. These personnel are attached to that forward unit for the duration of the mission.

Hip shot. An expression for a mission in which the artillery piece is set up, sited, and ready to shoot very quickly.

IS (immediate suppression) Mission. An artillery mission where the guns shoot immediately and quickly at a target in response to an FO's request for artillery support.

Key volunteer. A family support system utilized by the Marine Corps in which the designated NOK (next of kin) to a deployed Marine has a contact on base where he or she can go for information.

LAR (light armored reconnaissance). A battalion made up of, and using, LAVs for reconnaissance and fire support.

LAV (light armored vehicle). An eight-wheeled, lightly armed vehicle, very fast, that is used for scouting and reconnaissance. It can carry various weapons platforms, such as TOWs and mortars, but the main weapon is a 25mm chain gun mounted in the turret. The LAV also carries a crew of scouts.

LoD (line of departure). The designated border crossing point between Kuwait and Iraq. Once the LoD is crossed, the attack has begun.

Main CP (command post). Where the battalion executive officer commands, along with his "B" command group.

M198 155mm Howitzer. The heavy howitzer used by the Marine Corps, which shoots a variety of 155mm dia. rounds.

MEB. Marine Expeditionary Brigade.

MEF. Marine Expeditionary Force.

MEU (Marine Expeditionary Unit). The basic "Rapid Reaction Force" fielded by the United States in its defense.

MRLS (multiple rocket launching system). A defense system that shoots many rockets quickly.

MOPP (mission-oriented protective posture) suit. The special charcoal-lined suit worn by the Marines to ward off NBC attacks. "Posture" refers to the level of protection the Marines are to take, for example, MOPP 1, means Marines carry the gear with them. The degree of readiness goes up to MOPP 4, which is when Marines must wear the entire suit, including gloves, gas mask, and overboots.

MREs (meals ready to eat). Pre-packaged meals supplied to Marines and other American troops to be eaten in the field. Also nicknamed as "Meals Ready to Excrete" as well as "Meals Rejected by Ethiopians."

NBC (nuclear/biological/chemical). Also nicknamed as "No Body Cares" by Marines.

OIF. Operation Iraqi Freedom.

Red Rain mission. Incoming enemy fire, which is tracked by a special radar unit that plots the enemy fire's location and enables Marine artillery to respond with counter battery fire.

Ring mount. A circular mount on the top of a Humvee in which is mounted a .50-caliber heavy machine gun.

SL3 components. Gear and equipment that is used with the howitzer, i.e. shovels, pics, sights, aiming posts.

TAA (tactical assault area). The designated area from which the invasion started.

TAC CP (tactical command post). The second command post, commanded by the battalion commander. Usually located very close to the front lines, yet located several hundred yards away from the Main CP. Should the TAC CP take casualties, command of the unit continues without interruption.

TOW (tube-launched, optically-tracked, wire-guided missile). The primary anti-armor weapon of the infantry.

XO. Executive Officer.

Recommended Reading

Alexander, Col. Joseph H. *A Fellowship of Valor*. New York: Harper Collins, 1997.

——————. *Utmost Savagery*. Annapolis, Maryland: Naval Institute Press, 1995.

Asprey, Robert. *At Belleau Wood*. Denton, Texas: University of North Texas Press, 1996.

Boot, Max. *The Savage Wars of Peace*. New York: Basic Books, 2002.

Friedman, Thomas. *Longitudes & Attitudes*. New York: Farrar, Straus, and Giroux, 2002.

——————. "Because We Could." *The New York Times*. 4 June 2003: Op-Ed page.

Leckie, Robert. *Strong Men Armed*. New York: Random House, 1962.

Levin, Dan. *From the Battlefield*. Annapolis, Maryland: Naval Institute Press, 1995.

Manchester, William. *Goodbye, Darkness*. New York: Little, Brown & Co., 1979.

Murphy, Edward. *Semper Fi Vietnam*. Novato, California: Presidio Press, 1997.

Prezelin, Bernard. *Combat Fleets of the World*. Annapolis, Maryland: The Naval Institute, 1993.

Russ, Martin. *Breakout*. New York: Penguin Books, 2000.

Sledge, E. B. *With the Old Breed*. Novato, California: Presidio Press, 1981.

United States Marine Corps. *Small Wars Manual*. Manhatten, Kansas: Sunflower University Press, 1940.

Acknowledgments

I could not have written this book without the extraordinary cooperation of the RCT-2 Marines and their wives, parents, and girlfriends. Regardless of rank, I have never met a more gracious and helpful group of individuals, and frankly, I wish I could have included more of the RCT-2 Marines in this project.

Interviews

Not only is there no existing historical data for this battle, but much of what I have written is published here for the first time, and therefore, I have used extensive interviews to gather the information presented here.

While I tried to be as respectful of their time and family life as possible, I want to acknowledge that many of my phone calls came at inopportune moments: for example, as I was trying to interview Top Santivasci, he was leaving for Alaska in order to conduct a week of Arctic weather weapons training; Chaps Ritchie was emailing me from his training in the Sierra Nevadas, and both Col. Starnes and Lt. Col. Grabowski took time from their classes at the Army War College in Carlisle, PA to read and critique my efforts.

Every interview I conducted was invaluable for setting up the time frame and character of this book. The heart of this story, however, came from each Charlie Battery Marine who graciously shared his memories and impressions. I am grateful for their time and willingness to work with me. Gentlemen—I thank you all.

In particular, I would like to recognize the following Charlie Battery Marines for their extraordinary efforts in allowing me to interview them over a period of several months: Cpl. Gaspar Aguila, Pvt. Paul Barr, LCpl. Sobola Bechu, Cpl. Michael Czombos, Cpl. Jorge Delarosa, Cpl. Ryan Gallagher, Cpl. Christopher Gault, Cpl. Geoffrey Goodson, Cpl. Cory Hebert,

LCpl. Philip Lubin, Cpl. Justin Noyes, Corpsman James Sanders, Cpl. Joshua Souza, LCpl. Joseph Turcotte, and LCpl. Carl Warren.

In addition, I'd like to make special mention of the officers and senior NCOs of Charlie Battery, 1/10. All these Marines had to be coaxed into talking; they didn't want their stories to detract from the stories of their Charlie Battery enlisted men: 1st Lt. Sean Shea, MSgt. Michael Santivasci, GySgt. Clay Lambert, and SSgt. John Fontenoy.

While the 1/10 Marine interviews revealed how the war unfolded for them before, during, and after Iraq, it was the interviews with their parents, wives, and girlfriends that fully conveyed the rigors of war on the home front. Thank you to the following family and friends of 1/10: Mr. Paul Czombos (father), Miss Laura Doggett (fiancée), Mrs. Christy Fontenoy (wife), Mrs. Sharon Goodson (mother), Mrs. Jamie McMillan (mother), Mrs. Becky Sanders (wife), Mrs. Lisa Santivasci (wife), Miss Leah Starner (fiance), Mrs. Nancy Turcotte (mother), and Mrs. Lucille Warren (mother).

Lastly, my interviews with LT John Doran (USN) & Mrs. Colleen Doran, Lt. Col. Paul Dunahoe, Lt. Col. Royal Mortenson, and Lt. Cmdr. Gordon Ritchie played an important role in completing this new chapter of U.S. Marine Corps history.

Special Recognition

Several Marines went beyond the call of duty to help me in this endeavor, and they deserve special recognition.

Master Sergeant Michael Santivasci—who provided me with some quiet corrections and advice, along with his views on what makes a good Marine, and for his unlimited time, patience, and friendship in helping edit this book.

Master Sergeant Anthony Cross, a great guy—who fielded a lot of my questions when I was too embarrassed to bother Top Santivasci yet again, and who helped me begin to understand more of what was involved in being a Marine infantryman at war.

Lieutenant Colonel Rick Grabowski, CO of 1/2—who provided me with an overview of the Battle of An Nasiriyah, as well as his commentary about the roles and behavior of the senior NCOs and enlisted men.

Mike Harbert, a former Marine Major and a good friend—who took the time to explain much of the nomenclature necessary to relate this story properly. Mike also provided a few quotations for chapters 1 & 3.

First Lieutenant Sean Shea—who provided me with an accurate time-line for my "Peacekeeping" chapter, along with specific commentary and corrections, all of which I appreciated receiving.

Colonel Glenn Starnes, CO of 1/10—who graciously took time both during the Christmas 2003 season and afterwards to read my manuscript and email several pages of his comments and corrections.

Major Neil Wilson, commander of our English brothers of Battery G, Para Brigade—who fielded my cold-call and responded most graciously to my requests for information on the British role in An Nasiriyah, as well as with contact details for his men. Cheers!

Editorial, Technical & Publishing Assistance

Dan Levin, Col. Joseph Alexander, and Edward Murphy—each Marine authors who I called cold, introduced myself, told them what I wanted to do, and begged for help. All of them were uniformly helpful to my initial plea for contacts in publishing.

Sergeant Spencer Harris and SSgt. Jay Connolly of the Camp Lejeune Media Office arranged all the interviews I needed. In particular, I'd like to thank Sgt. Harris for his unfailing courtesy and assistance, regardless of how last-minute or odd my requests or questions were.

Thank you to my friends, Mary and Neil Ross and Jeff Parker, who read my drafts, made plenty of comments, didn't laugh out loud, and who then got me squared away on how to write this book.

My friend, Jeff Parker, deserves a special mention for the work he did regarding the photos and maps. Jeff supplied all the technical expertise that made the maps and website as good as they are.

My friend of 35 years, Chuck Richardson, badgered me daily to finish this book, and then let me print numerous copies of my numerous drafts off his laser printer so I could send them out to people for their comments and corrections. His editorial feedback and moral support helped make this book possible.

The Kuwait and Middle Eastern maps and raw data came from the Kuwait Information Office section of the Kuwaiti Embassy in Washington. Ms. Lana Boustany and Ms. Fatma Ah Al-Khalifa were most helpful in providing me with the information I requested.

My thanks to my aunt, Sister Alice Lubin, of the Sisters of Mercy, College of St. Elizabeth. Aunt Alice went through my various drafts with a red pen, like the former head of the English Department she is. Who needs spell check and grammar check when you have a semi-retired nun as your proofreader?

And to my editor, Vickie Reierson, who would let me rant about why each word was so important, and then proceed to calmly explain why things need to be changed. Not only did I listen to her, but I also learned from her.

Accommodations

Kathy Hawkins of the MICROTEL, Commerce Road, Jacksonville, North Carolina (910-455-4142)—who loaned me the conference room, and then picked up a lot of empty Charlie Battery beer bottles without excessive complaint!

Photo Contributions

The photos in this book hailed from a number of personal collections. These visual representations enhanced and personalized the story of Charlie Battery and 1/10 in ways the written word cannot. Thank you to the following people for their permission to reprint their photographs in this publication: Pvt. Paul Barr, Cpl. Michael Czombos, Cpl. Jorge Delarosa, Lt. Col. Rick Grabowski, Cpl. Cory Hebert, LCpl. Philip Lubin, Corpsman James Sanders, 1st Lt. Sean Shea, Miss Leah Starner, and Lockheed-Martin/ Avondale Shipyard (USS *Ashland* photos).